Myths and
Legends of the
Martial Arts
Π

Myths and Legends of the Martial Arts

Π

Peter Lewis

PRION

First published in 1998 in Great Britain by
Prion Books Limited
Imperial Works, Perren Street,
London NW5 3EP

Reprinted 1999

ISBN 1-85375-271-1

Cover design by Bob Eames
Cover image courtesy of The Bridgeman Art Library
Printed and bound in Great Britain
by Creative Print & Design, Wales

'The dance of life goes on,
nothing in the Universe stands still'

Contents

Contents

Introduction

Π

There is an old Chinese proverb which states: 'A story grows bigger by the telling.'

Much of what purports to be history within martial arts has been handed down verbally rather than scripted. Consequently, the truth becomes corrupted and facts tend to follow the fancy of whomsoever is telling the story. The truth is further tainted with embellishments from the storyteller's own imagination. A veritable pot pourri of fact mixed together with a great deal of fiction distances the tale from its origins and the truth of actual events. Be that as it may, there is still a nucleus of original information within every myth, and this allows us to gather enough facts in order to understand, as well as to enjoy, it centuries later.

Translations of Southeast Asian manuscripts can often obscure more than they clarify. They say repetition eventually gives validity, and indeed the tales and legends are so often repeated that they have to be assessed upon their merit and given the benefit of the doubt. Some are just tales that got bigger by the telling. Whether or not the storytellers of old kept to the facts is of little consequence to us today. This book, although written purely for entertainment, does contain within the stories epigrams of ancient Oriental wisdom that still have something to say about how to live in our modern, technological age.

When writing about the distant and recent past in the Asian world, the Western reader has to be aware of the vastly different religious, cultural and political factors of the times. If not, and the reader does not accept the events in the stories, then a curtain is drawn that will prevent the reader from enjoying the stories for what they are – pure and simple. All too often, as Kipling so famously wrote, 'East is East and West is West and ne'er the twain shall meet.'

Much of the history of the martial arts is steeped in Oriental philosophies which span some 3,000 years. A story may not seem to have a point to it, but upon closer examination, by looking a little deeper, the essence of the tale will appear. An Asian reading Greek mythology for the very first time would find many of the stories quite preposterous. We must show respect to Asia's venerable traditions of folklore and fable and accept the stories just as they have been handed down.

Some of the legends related in this book will conjure tales of ancient kung fu masters founding the first principles of a fighting system that eventually lead to a true and systematised martial arts discipline. For example, 'Painting Legs on a Snake' is a story about making positive decisions, and 'Overflowing Cup' is a little tale that emphasises the point about learning and wisdom. The mix of material within a story is quite diverse because the intention is to cover the many aspects that make up the martial arts. Man, nature, religion and the universe all play an integral part in the Asian pantheon and for the most part run parallel with the founding and development of martial disciplines, and their underlying theme of thought immersed in philosophy.

Wisdom, wit, heroism and strength in adversity are just some of the many aspects to be found in the stories, along with the historical events that inspired the early beginnings of the martial arts.

§

The Nature
of a
Man

Π

Many years ago, in the Honan province of northern China, there was a hung gar school presided over by a master whose secret techniques of fighting had been handed down from father to son, generation after generation. The master hoped that when his only son was competent enough he would take over the running of the school. His son was indeed adept at many of the techniques within the system and could be classed as the top fighter in the school. However, he had no skill as a teacher and could not explain the system to the students.

The father worried that when his son took over the teaching many of the secret techniques, some over 200 years old, would eventually be forgotten. The son lacked patience with the slower members of the school, and seemed only to have time for the best fighters. One day his father asked him why it was that he only instructed the good fighters. To which the son replied that he couldn't be bothered with the students who were too slow at learning the techniques. It was much more exciting teaching the accomplished fighters, because he could see the results of his tuition almost immediately.

The father explained to him that everyone has a different nature which is born within them and cannot be changed. Although some pupils learn quicker than others, it is sometimes the slower student who turns out to be the more competent. He also pointed out that once the better fighters became too old to fight they would leave and take up other, less strenuous pursuits. He would then be left alone because the students he did not want to teach would eventually lose interest and also leave. Consequently, their 200-year-old family system of kung fu would simply fade away.

Being a good fighter is not what kung fu is all about, stated his father, and went on to explain the philosophy that goes hand in hand with the techniques. Wisdom, patience and a clear understanding of each student's needs is what makes a good teacher. We are all born unique and it is wrong to mould a student into something he is not. To try to do so would be against his nature and this is not the way of kung fu. He could see that his son was finding it difficult to understand what he was saying, so he told him the story about a frog and a scorpion in the hope that it would illustrate more clearly what he wanted his son to understand.

One day a scorpion arrived at the bank of a river he wanted to cross, but there was no bridge. He asked a frog that was sitting nearby if he would take him across the river on his back. The frog refused because he thought that the scorpion would sting him. The scorpion replied that it would be foolish to sting the frog because then they would both drown. The frog could see the logic in this and so agreed to carry, but about halfway across the scorpion stung the frog which immediately died, drowning the scorpion in the process.

The kung fu master's son looked up at his father, expecting there would be more to the story, but there wasn't any more. The son said that he didn't understand why the scorpion had stung the frog. The father replied that stinging and killing are what a scorpion does – that is its nature. The scorpion is not to blame because it had no choice. You cannot change the nature of anything, he went on to say. One student may be slower at learning than another, but that doesn't make the faster student a better fighter or a better person. Each student develops and acts according to his nature. The son at last understood what his father meant and from that day on he taught all the students to the best of his ability, thus preserving the family system of kung fu.

§

The Master Swordsman

Π

The Japanese swordsman Miyamoto Musashi was the greatest who ever lived. Known today as the 'Sword Saint', there are many tales of his great exploits. One such story tells of Musashi when he was just a young boy, about twelve years old. He had spent years practising with a wooden sword and now felt, even at his young age, ready for a challenge match.

His opportunity came when a local swordsman named Kihei, whom many thought of as the greatest fighter in the district, came to Musashi's village laying down challenges to the local samurai. Fearing Kihei's reputation, many samurai arranged to be in other districts at the time of his visit. To refuse a challenge would cause great loss of face and be the ultimate act of cowardice for a samurai.

Whilst Kihei was in the marketplace calling for the samurai to come out and fight him, the small but sturdy frame of Musashi stepped forward and accepted the challenge to fight. Kihei looked at the boy with the wooden sword and laughed out loud. He said that he would squash him like an ant unless he cleared off, and with that spat upon Musashi. In the blink of an eye, Musashi, taking advantage of Kihei's moment of unpreparedness, sprung into action. With the speed of a cobra, he brought his wooden sword crashing down upon Kihei's skull. Kihei was taken completely by surprise and fell to the ground with his skull split open like a melon. Musashi then commenced to pulverise his head until it was pulp. Legend relates that he then turned around and calmly walked away, leaving in his wake Kihei's battered body and the beginning of a legend.

In just a few years Musashi's reputation grew and soon he was the most feared swordsman in all Japan. He never ceased to study, constantly improving his knowledge of fighting and strategy and the principles of attack and defence. Musashi now felt ready to take on the great Seijuro Sensei who was master of a sword school in Kyoto, and reputedly the greatest of all the sword fighters.

In those days challenges to the head of a school of martial arts were always taken up by the senior students. In this way the master of the school would not himself lose face if his student was defeated. Musashi therefore worked out a plan to make sure that it was Seijuro who accepted his challenge and not one of his students. He openly declared in the marketplace of the city that he wanted to fight Seijuro Sensei and that if he didn't come out and meet him he was a coward. He also had posters printed up announcing that Seijuro Sensei would meet Miyamoto Musashi in a fight to the death, with the place, date and time also provided.

This was too much for Seijuro. Even though the senior students begged him to let them go in his place Seijuro was now so angry that he would let nothing stand in the way of his teaching this impudent young fighter a lethal lesson. At the appointed time and date Seijuro Sensei was duly waiting for his challenger to appear. The code of the samurai dictated that in such a contest all points of formal etiquette should be observed, and so as dawn broke, the appointed hour of the fight, Seijuro stood on the dusty field in all his samurai splendour. Virtually the entire population of the city had turned out to watch the fight.

Two hours later Seijuro was still there but Musashi had not yet appeared. A further two hours elapsed but still the challenger did not show. By now Seijuro was getting impatient and was beginning to relax from the sombre pose of his fighting stance. But Musashi was in fact no more than ten yards away dressed as a local peasant and standing unnoticed in the crowd. As afternoon turned to early evening the normally composed Seijuro was visibly enraged. It was at this moment that Musashi strolled out from the crowd. Seijuro was shocked to see such an insultingly scruffy opponent at this most formal occasion, and further agitated that Musashi was armed only with his wooden practice sword. Totally overwhelmed with rage Seijuro drew his sword. As the huge, long sword arced its way downwards, Musashi lifted his wooden sword in an upward sweeping motion and crashed it under Seijuro's chin. The impact killed Seijuro instantly.

Seijuro died because he forgot two of the most important elements of Zen philosophy, namely to have a clear mind and to focus exclusively upon the task at hand. His impatience and rage because Musashi had not complied with formality and arrived so very late dressed like a peasant had upset him beyond reason. Musashi knew that an angry fighter has an angry mind, and an angry mind knows no skill or discipline.

Painting Legs on a Snake

Π

There was once a great kung fu master who was in the autumn of his years, and tradition dictated that he had to hand down all the secret knowledge of his kung fu style to his most senior student. However, seniority in this instance was not just a question of time served. The problem the master was faced with was that he had two students of equal skill. In order to choose between them he set them a test. He ordered both students to go outside and each draw an animal in the dirt. The student who drew an animal the fastest and one which was instantly recognisable by the master would inherit all.

Each grabbing a stick, the students quickly set to work. The first student's instinct was to quickly draw an elongated letter 'S' in the dirt. He then looked up and saw that the second student was still drawing.

Feeling worried that he had perhaps been too quick, he began to embellish his drawing by adding a series of squiggles meant to represent legs. As he was about to add a third leg the other student straightened up, indicating that he had finished his drawing. The master walked over and proclaimed the second student the winner.

Turning to the first student, he asked, 'Tell me, why did you carry on after you had finished drawing in the sand what was quite obviously a snake?'

The student replied, 'Because Master, having thought of a snake and drawn it so quickly, I then had doubts whether or not you would recognise what it was supposed to be. Therefore I put legs on it so that it would resemble a lizard.'

'The doubt in your mind and the hesitation you displayed', explained the master, 'cost you the position as the next master of the style.'

From that time on, the saying, 'Don't paint legs on a snake,' has been used when it would be pointless to try and improve upon something that is already perfectly adequate.

§

The Shaolin Temple

Π

It is often disputed that because such a wide variety of martial arts styles exists in China they should all have originated at the Shaolin Temple in Hunan province. What is perhaps nearer to the truth is that there were a number of temples throughout China where warrior monks trained in combat styles. The Shaolin monastery (Shaolin means 'small wood' or 'little forest') was built around AD 495 by imperial decree of the Emperor Hsiao–Wen and lies at the foot of the Song Shan mountains. It was probably the forerunner of later establishments elsewhere in the country, which were founded by Shaolin priests who had qualified and gone out into the world. Therefore various martial traditions were nurtured and underwent subtle changes, emerging as subdivisions of the major styles. Each style was named after the priest or monk who initiated the changes.

Two hundred years after its founding the first Emperor of the T'ang dynasty, T'ai Tsung, appealed to the fighting monks for a force to help him defeat General Wang-Shih-Ch'ung, who was attempting to establish a separate regime. The Shaolin monks went to the aid of their Emperor and together they defeated Wang.

Legend states that 13 monks gave their assistance, but in reality it was perhaps a much larger force, as the monastery was known to house at least 500 fighting monks. In recognition of their great deeds the Emperor conferred upon Shaolin the title 'Number One Monastery Under Heaven'.

In 1674 the Shaolin monks were called upon again by an Emperor to provide a contingent of warrior monks. This time by the Ch'ing Emperor K'ang–Hsi. Scrolls from the period tell of how these monks fought seven and ten men at a time, defeating all who came in their path. Their skill was such that the Emperor commented, 'Give me ten thousand of these monks and I will conquer the world.'

After the war the monks returned to Shaolin to resume their religious life. Moves were afoot, however, at the imperial court to undermine the favour and patronage the Emperor showed to the monks. Through petty jealousies and vicious plotting by

Hunan landowners and lords, the Emperor was eventually persuaded that such a force, with its amazing expertise in the art of combat and strategy, would one day prove to be a threat to the throne and should therefore be disbanded.

The Emperor half-heartedly gave way to the land-grabbing nobles and a huge army was mustered. Aided by a renegade Shaolin monk, the Emperor's army attacked the monastery and after many months of fighting razed it to the ground. It is said that only five monks managed to escape this carnage and fled to the Yellow River to evade capture. These monks are known as the five ancestors and considered to be the legendary founders of China's notorious secret society, the Triads.

The Shaolin monastery still exists and attracts tourists from all over the world. It has been extensively rebuilt by the Chinese People's Republic and is preserved as a historic monument. Monks still live and work there, and practise their kung fu techniques daily, though their kung fu style now is more gymnastic than lethal.

§

The Karate Man and the Tiger

Π

Gogen Yamaguchi, the founder of the goju-kai style of karate, had many adventures as a young man and one of the most famous occurred during World War II. The Japanese government had sent Yamaguchi to Manchuria on secret business, and whilst conducting certain negotiations he was captured by forces of the Kuomintang (the Chinese National People's Party) government. They shipped him off to a labour camp where he was treated very badly and suffered great hardship and deprivation.

Although a model prisoner who did everything he was told, Yamaguchi's captors were wary of him. There was something in his demeanour, the way he walked proudly and the way the other prisoners held him in such high regard which caused the guards to be almost afraid of him.

The normal day's routine for the prisoners was to eat whatever was available, which was never enough, and then to lounge about either sleeping or gossiping. But Yamaguchi did not behave as the other prisoners. When he was allowed out of his cell, he would run around the exercise area and practise all manner of kicks and punches hour after hour. In his cell he would sit and meditate for long periods. Yamaguchi refused to bow down and be broken by the conditions of his imprisonment.

The guards began to see this proud Japanese as something of a superhuman being. He always looked fit and healthy unlike the other prisoners, and yet he ate the same starvation diet. They began to think of him as a demon and their fear grew. News soon reached the camp commandant's office of this strange prisoner. On further investigation it was discovered who he was and orders were issued that at all costs he must be broken, so that he would lose face before the other prisoners.

Yamaguchi was placed in solitary confinement and his rations would have barely kept a child alive. For twenty hours a day he sat in his cell in total darkness. The cell was so small that when he sat cross-legged his knees touched the walls. Daily beatings by the guards still failed to affect him or break his spirit. Each day he would practise his special breathing exercises and then put himself into a trance-like state so that he felt neither pain nor hunger. The prison officials could not believe that one man could withstand such harsh treatment and still remain fit and unbroken. By now rumour was rife around the camp about the demon man who's very name seemed to frighten the guards when it was whispered by the prisoners.

The commandant finally ordered an ultimate test that would rid them of this man once and for all. They dragged Yamaguchi out of his cell and walked him across the compound to where there was a cage containing a half-starved tiger. Laughing, the guards pushed him into the cage and ordered the whole camp to watch the Japanese karate man being eaten alive. 'Let's see your karate help you now,' goaded one of the guards.

The minute Yamaguchi was pushed into the cage a strange look came into his eyes. He adopted a karate stance and with an ear-piercing yell he attacked the tiger. The animal was momentarily stunned by the shout, so allowing enough time for Yamaguchi to jump on to its back and apply a strangulation technique from behind. In the process he let out another screeching yell right into the tiger's ear and then pulled back on his arms, using every bit of strength in his body. Moments later the tiger slumped to the cage floor, dead. The guards looked terrified and ran off, leaving Yamaguchi in the cage overnight with the dead tiger.

The next morning he was let out of the cell and allowed to rejoin the other prisoners. Less than two weeks later he was exchanged with another political prisoner, thus facilitating his release. The guards at the camp breathed a sigh of relief when this demon karate man left the camp.

Years later, when near to death, Yamaguchi was asked what karate was all about. He replied, 'Karate is not about fighting; it is about truth.'

§

Five Against One

Π

The island of Okinawa, in the Ryukyu Archipelago off the coast of Japan, is said to be where karate as we know it today has its roots. Many styles of karate from Okinawa changed slightly when they reached the Japanese mainland. However, one of the styles that remains purely Okinawan is uechi-ryu, which was founded by Kanbun Uechi. Kanbun Uechi took his own indigenous karate and added elements of Chinese kung fu from the styles of the Tiger, Dragon and Crane. The Chinese name for this system was termed pangai-noon, which means 'half hard, half soft'.

Kanbun Uechi as a foreigner in China was picked upon often and his many victories in fights created an aura of invincibility. One day he went to visit a friend who lived as a recluse deep in the forest. As evening fell Kanbun bade farewell to his friend and began the long walk home. Halfway home he was suddenly confronted by five tough-looking bandits, who threatened that if he had no money they would take his clothes, and if he did not argue they would let him live. When Kanbun Uechi refused to disrobe, one of the bandits rushed at him. Calmly stepping aside, Kanbun deflected the blow and then like lightning struck back. The bandit leader fell dead at his feet. The other four bandits looked on in amazement. Kanbun told them to pick up their leader and dispose of him. He then asked politely if any of them wanted to still try to take his clothes, but there was no response. Kanbun told the bandits that he had enjoyed the little confrontation because he had been getting bored walking home alone. He said to them that from now on he would be travelling this way home every night, and so the next time they wanted to attack him perhaps they would try and surprise him. That way, Kanbun went on, it would be more of a challenge to defend himself. He then turned and continued his journey home.

Kanbun Uechi travelled that same path every night for a week, but he was never again troubled with bandits.

The Waiter
and the
Seaman

Π

Just after World War II, in the Malaysian town of
Telok, a young, shy, half-Chinese youth was waiting tables in a busy restaurant in order to earn
enough money to feed his mother and sisters. The
waiter, whose name was Leong, had left the village
where he had lived for eighteen years in search of
work.

He had spent his formative years, during the
Japanese occupation, learning kung fu from the
monks in the temple opposite his house. He became
so adept at the techniques of kung fu that the senior
monks felt that the young Leong was surely a great
fighter in the making. When he was only twelve years
old he had fought in a local tournament and beaten
men twice his size. He was expected to go far and
one day perhaps become a professional fighter.

The Waiter and the Seaman

One evening the restaurant was full of rowdy servicemen drinking and shouting, and one particular drunk was staggering about insulting everybody and spilling beer as he went. Spying the young Leong hurrying around the tables he began to hurl insults at the lad. Leong just ignored him and carried on with his work. The drunk did not give up, however, and bringing in some of his friends from the bar they surrounded Leong and insisted that he drink with them. The boy still ignored them and collected up the plates from the empty tables.

The drunk then turned nasty and grabbed Leong by his shirt and tried to force a mug of beer into his mouth. At this stage three of the drunken seaman's friends egged their pal on, shouting, 'Make the Chinese drink it all'. Leong, sensing that threats were about to turn to violence, quickly sprang to the side with his back to the wall facing the four men, his fighting instinct welling up inside him.

The seaman who had been doing all the shouting lifted up his heavy glass mug with the intention of smashing it into the boy's face. Like a rocket Leong moved in and executed a footsweep that was so hard the drunk was lifted three feet into the air and came crashing down in a mess of broken glass and tables. His friends attacked as one, their hands clawing at the boy. Leong sensed where the immediate danger was and struck one sailor with a front kick to the groin that finished him instantly. Barely had his foot withdrawn before a second sailor was on him only to be met with an elbow to the throat that sent him back choking for breath. The third seaman now faced Leong with one hand outstretched before him. He was holding a vicious-looking filleting knife of the type that most sailors carried. Warily, Leong looked at the deadly blade and when the seaman lunged he sidestepped at the same time, without losing sight of the blade. As the seaman went past him, Leong grabbed the knife arm and twisted the wrist using a finger and thumb. A crack was heard, the knife fell to the floor as did the seaman, screaming 'My wrist is broken!'

The fight was over and the diners, who in their panic had fled the restaurant, began to return to their tables. The police arrived and upon hearing the story escorted the injured sailors out of the restaurant. The people clapped the young Leong for his superb actions, and when the restaurant closed he found that he had received far more in tips than he usually did. Even today they still tell the tale of the young waiter who used kung fu to defeat ten six-foot sailors with knives. After all, in the words of the Chinese proverb, 'A story grows bigger by the telling'.

Beautiful Springtime

II

In the province of Yunan in southern China there lived a lovely young woman called Yim Wing Chun. She was in love with her childhood sweetheart Leong Bok Chao. Leong had gone away to work and in his absence Yim was making all the necessary preparations for their forthcoming marriage.

In the mountains above her village there lived a bandit who had seen Yim and wanted her for himself, even though he knew she was betrothed to another. He sent his men to the village and they made threats to Yim and her father, saying that unless she broke off the engagement and married the bandit chief bad things would happen to her and her family. There was no consoling Yim because she knew that if she did not marry the brigand he would kill her father and take her anyway. One day whilst out collecting wood for the fire Yim was crying about everything that had befallen her. A passing nun named Ng Mui heard Yim's weeping and went to see if there was anything she could do to help.

After Yim had explained her problem, the nun told her not to worry as she had a plan. First of all Yim had to send a letter to Leong Bok Chao to call off the engagement for one year, saying that she wanted to seek guidance through the temple. Yim's father then told the brigand that Yim had broken off her engagement and that now she was free to marry, but not for one year as she was looking for spiritual guidance. The bandit laughed with glee because he thought that he had won Yim's hand.

Now, Ng Mui was a Shaolin nun and an expert in the mui fa chuan ('plum flower fist') system of kung fu, and it was said that she was one of the survivors of the sacking of the Shaolin monastery. By her ruse she had gained enough time for her to instruct Yim in all the fighting techniques of the system. Hour after hour, day after day, Yim trained hard, and by learning on a one-to-one basis she was able to perfect the fighting skills at a much faster rate than normal. She had grasped all the advanced techniques of the plum flower fist system within six months. But she felt uncomfortable with many of the moves as she thought them too complex and relied too much on power techniques. She searched through the scrolls at the temple to find another system perhaps better suited to a woman's strength and capabilities. However, not finding anything suitable she began to experiment with what she already knew.

She changed strikes and kicks to match her own stature. Strength blows were substituted for subtle body manoeuvres. Eventually, through continued experimentation, she developed her own style of fighting which was based upon direct line attacks, working on the principle that a straight line is the shortest distance between two objects. Under the guidance of Ng Mui, Yim finally arrived at total competence in a system that achieved her aims exactly.

The year passed and Yim left the temple and went back to live with her father. She had him put posters up around the town which stated she would marry anyone who could beat her in hand-to-hand combat. She also had her father spread the rumour that she had trained in kung fu all her life. When the brigand heard what was going on he and his gang came down from the mountains in order to beat the 'little girl' up and claim her as his bride. The fight was held in the town square and all the villagers came to watch. The brigand charged at Yim in order to overwhelm her, but she just hit him hard in the throat when he came within range. Getting up, his pride and throat badly bruised, he charged even harder at the girl. Yim caught him with an open palm strike to the nose and down he went again. The brigand became even more enraged and with blood streaming down his face he charged again, but this time kicked out at Yim with a front kick. His kicked missed but Yim's didn't, though it seemed that she hadn't moved at all, such was the subtlety of her new style. She caught the brigand full on the side of the knee breaking his leg and he fell to the ground screaming in pain.

Yim had won the day and the brigand had to be helped back home by his men, losing so much face that he never attempted to intimidate her again. Yim Wing Chun immediately sent a letter to Leong Bok Chao asking him to come back and marry her. Yim dedicated this new style to Ng Mui, but named the style after herself, Wing Chun, which translates as 'Beautiful Springtime'. It is the only kung fu style invented by a woman. The nucleus of this style was the first kung fu system learned by Bruce Lee.

Iron
Belly
Shang

∏

Hsing-i (pronounced shing-ee) is one of the internal kung fu systems which stress the development of the internal energy known as chi, rather than pure muscular strength. There is a story about one of the great warriors of hsing-i, a man named Shang Yun-hsiang, who was born in the Shantung province of China. Because his family were very poor he never learned to read or write. The great passion in his life was his kung fu training, and he had the great fortune to be taught by the great hsing-i master Li Tsun-i.

Young Shang would walk to the school, a distance of over twenty miles, each day. He would lift up rocks and carry them in his outstretched arms as he walked in order to build up his strength. Sometimes rather than use a bridge to cross a river he would swim across. Shang did everything he could to develop his body. By the time he was twenty years old he was not only a great fighter but also as strong as an ox, both mentally and physically.

He was now a master of hsing-i and opened a school in a large town. It is said that when he went through the basic movements of hsing-i for his students the building used to shake. Everyone knew that the powerhouse of his great strength was his stomach. He was once caught up in a fight at a local tavern during which one of his opponents grabbed him around the waist, but using the power of his paunch Shang broke his attacker's wrists.

Another story relates that whilst visiting a boxing gym he was approached by a senior student and asked if it was true that his stomach was like an iron wall. He agreed to let the student hit him in the stomach. But the student asked Shang to remain seated, thinking that Shang would therefore not be able to summon up all his strength from his legs. So Shang sat there as the student unleashed his best possible punch at his stomach. At the very last moment, just as the student's fist was about to impact, Shang suddenly raised a hand, palm open, so that the student struck the palm rather than his stomach. This was not to block the strike from the student, but because Shang had concentrated his internal energy through his body and into his palm just to see what would happen when a blow hit his hand. The student was hurled back through the air more than thirty feet, crashing through a door into the yard. Shang's internal energy had generated unseen power through the palm of his hand, propelled the student backwards with more than ten times the energy he had used in his punch. Such is the power of chi energy.

Although a naturally great fighter who was never beaten, Shang was not very intelligent and lacked the mental ability to teach his art. Many students flocked to his school attempting to learn the great and mysterious art of hsing-i, but Shang was unable to teach and explain the subtle points of developing and using the intrinsic energy of chi. He could only demonstrate, and never explain how the system worked. His powers were so great that many of his students died at his hands trying to learn the art. The students eventually gave up on Shang – a man so powerful that it was said 'he would fight a bear and give it first bite'.

§

The Master
of
Strategy

∏

In China during the period known as the Warring
States, around 500 BC, a great Chinese general and
military strategist named Sun Tsu wrote a book on
warfare called *The Art of War*. It is a treatise on the
exact science of such subjects as offensive strategy,
weaknesses and strengths of the enemy, terrain, use of
spies, guerrilla warfare and vulnerability. Mere numbers alone, Sun Tsu stated, conferred no advantage.
He did not conceive of war in terms of slaughter and
destruction, but believed that an objective should and
could be taken with the proper use of strategy and
sound information of the enemy's plans. He always
cautioned his Emperor not to place reliance on sheer
military power.

Once during discussions at the imperial court,
Sun Tsu claimed that given the right directive and

motivation anyone could be trained as a complete fighting unit within an army. The many generals gathered at the court laughed at this audacious claim. 'This man is just a military advisor, what does he know about real fighting?' The emperor asked Sun Tsu if he really meant what he had said about turning anyone into a soldier. Sun Tsu nodded and added, 'As long as you agree that I will have complete control during the training and no interference from anyone.'

The Emperor therefore set Sun Tsu a test by ordering him to turn one hundred of his concubines into a drilled military unit. The Emperor ordered the women into the courtyard, followed closely by the grinning generals who felt that Sun Tsu had been cleverly tricked and had no chance of successfully completing the task. Sun Tsu tried to get the women to form lines in single file, one line behind the other, but they just giggled and began pushing and shoving each other. The generals thought this spectacle good entertainment and laughed along with the concubines. Sun Tsu explained to the Emperor that perhaps the women had not understood his orders because they had not been explicit enough. Once more he told the women what he wanted them to do, and again they laughed, waved at the generals and could not form one straight line let alone four as Sun Tsu had ordered. All in all, it was a total disaster.

Sun Tsu stepped forward and selected two of the concubines and ordered them to be beheaded. The Emperor jumped up and protested, because these two particular concubines happened to be his favourites. But Sun Tsu replied, 'You did say, sire, that I would have complete control.' The Emperor could not go back on his word and so the deed was done. The other women just looked on in a state of shock. The threat of death and the reality of it actually being carried out on two of their own had the desired effect. Now, when Sun Tsu issued his orders the women quietly and quickly obeyed them to the letter. No more giggling and laughing was heard in the courtyard. The women filed off in four lines, one behind the other. For the next two hours Sun Tsu put them through basic military commands that were obeyed instantly. The generals just stared in disbelief as the palace concubines were turned into well-disciplined troops. Sun Tsu had proved his point.

§

Stick
versus
Sword

II

The stick does not conjure up the same glamour as other weapons of the martial arts, and yet Muso Gonnosuke defeated the greatest swordsman in all Japan armed only with a simple stick. This must surely prove that it is the man behind the weapon and not the weapon itself that is the critical factor. One of the popular stick schools in Japan is that of the Shindo Muso Ryu. Their core weapon is a four-foot long stick called a jo. The wood for a jo is not kiln-dried but allowed to dry naturally, as kiln-drying takes out too much of the natural water content, leaving the wood light and brittle. The jo is about an inch thick and very strong. In fact when jodo ('way of the stick') is used against a live blade, a jo is capable of either shattering or bending it.

Muso Gonnosuke was a master of the bo staff (a

six-foot pole) and famous throughout Japan. He would constantly fight in contests against swordsmen and other weapons experts and never once was he defeated. That was until he met the Sword Saint himself, Miyamoto Musashi.

They met on a field outside the city of Edo, which is present-day Tokyo, in a contest of supreme skill. At one point Muso Gonnosuke struck downwards with his bo staff which was immediately caught in the cross block of Musashi's two swords (fighting with two swords had become Musashi's hallmark). Unable to retrieve his staff locked in the steel grip of the two swords without putting himself in danger, Gonnosuke had no idea what he was going to do next. However, Musashi, knowing of Gonnosuke's fame as a fighter and chivalrous man, refused to press home his advantage and spared his life. Muso Gonnosuke left the field happy to be alive yet annoyed that he had lost for the first time in his life.

For the next few years Gonnosuke searched far and wide in an attempt to find a technique that could beat Musashi's two-sword style. He decided to spend some time in meditation, so he retired to a mountain and reflected upon life and his martial art. He lived an austere life of rigid discipline, often fasting for days at a time. One night he had a dream in which he believed that divine guidance showed him what he must do. The next day he searched for a white oak tree and cut off a branch and fashioned a staff. But this time it would be a lot shorter than his six-foot bo staff. It had been revealed in his dream that he should make a lighter and shorter weapon with a smaller diameter. Eventually it was finished. Gonnosuke had made a much lighter, four-foot stick which he called a jo stick.

Gonnosuke then developed new movements that suited wielding the much shorter stick. He found that the shorter stick allowed him to get in much closer than he could with the old bo staff. He also developed a system for striking at the vital points of the body called atemi. After two years of training Gonnosuke felt that he had perfected the jo art and was ready to try it in combat. News quickly spread that armed with his shorter stick he could defeat anyone who came against him. Naturally, Musashi got to hear of this and a few months later the two protagonists faced each other once more.

The return match was a very different affair from the first. Musashi, try as he would, could not better Gonnosuke. Then, just as it looked as though an impasse had been reached, Gonnosuke struck and clearly defeated Musashi, for the first and only time in his life. Gonnosuke spared his life, however, just as Musashi has spared his.

The
Rebel
Monk

Π

One day, in a monastery a few miles from the city of Peking, a monk was tending his vegetable garden when he noticed a crane pecking at his recently planted crops. The monk, named Hung, was a master of the Tiger system of kung fu. He picked up his long-handled spade and proceeded to shoo the bird away, but no matter which way he struck the crane eluded the blows. He put the spade down and went to get his long monk's staff, then he began in earnest to try and strike the bird. The crane seemed only intent upon eating and treated Hung as if he was incidental to the feeding process. Hung swung one way and then another with his long staff, but each time the bird avoided the blow and then coun-terattacked, beating its wings down upon the monk. When the bird had had enough to eat it flew off, leaving the Tiger master quite amazed.

That night in his room the monk began to ponder upon the actions he had taken to shoo the bird away. Taking some paper, he wrote down what he could remember of the manoeuvres the crane had made to avoid being hit. Hung then decided that he would take further notes the next time he saw the bird. Two days later the crane came back to the garden to indulge itself yet again. This time the monk attacked in a prescribed fashion, and every arc and angle of attack was duly noted and so too was the bird's response. Eventually, over a period of weeks, the monk had collected detailed notes on every conceivable point of attack and the bird's defence. He consequently incorporated his findings into his own fighting system. The Crane and Tiger system was named after him and became known as hung gar.

The style was further developed some years later when Hung got involved with a revolutionary group after he had left the monastery. During the late 19th century, the Chinese had become increasingly resentful of Western intervention and exploitation of their country, and an intense hatred of all Westerners or Gweilos ('white devils') began to develop. Hung got involved with political intrigues and as a kung fu master was looked upon as a leader and many people rallied to his name. Pretty soon he was on the run from both the Western powers and the Manchu government.

He became involved with the I Ho Chuan (Fist of Righteous Harmony) secret society, which advocated war to drive the Westerners out of China. The society felt that they should look to the old ways of battle and encouraged the people to fight back using their kung fu heritage as a weapon. Hung trained thousands and thousands of Chinese peasants in the ways of his style. But he had to go into hiding when warrants for his arrest were issued. It seemed that the government had spies everywhere and Hung was only ever one step in front of the soldiers. It was suggested he take refuge in a nearby port where there were thousands of junks anchored in the bay. So Hung went to the port and sheltered in the so-called floating city.

He was certainly safe in his hiding place but his training began to suffer. Living in a low-roofed junk all day meant that there was no room for the daily practice of his kung fu techniques. He was informed that if he were to remain free, however, then he must endure his cramped confinement. Hung then began to play around with the techniques of his Tiger Crane system, and slowly he developed the low, crouching horse stance called ma-pu, which meant that he developed very strong legs and an awesome kicking power. Using this stance, he was able to introduce new and more powerful techniques into his style.

By now the seething hatred of the Western powers was at explosion point, but the Dowager Empress did not seem to want to get involved. Then, in 1900, the kung fu men, who had blind obedience to their leaders and superhuman faith in their fighting skills, suddenly erupted and attacked Westerners all over China – the Boxer Uprising had begun.

Chinese dressed in white and wearing red turbans attacked anyone and anything remotely connected with the Westerners. Many troops were brought in by the Western powers in order to stop the violence. The British troops when faced with thousands of screaming Chinese waving their fists in the air nicknamed them 'boxers'. The kung fu men were indoctrinated to believe that they were invulnerable to bullets, swords or knives. Their leaders performed incredible feats to prove this was true. The simple Chinese peasants were gullible and, aided by trickery, the rebel leaders convinced them to ignore the Westerners' guns, which of course resulted in many deaths. The few short months of the revolt culminated in the siege of the British legation at Peking.

Although the uprising was over, Hung was still a wanted man and so he fled to the mountains. What became of him after that is not known. As for his style of hung gar, the many students he trained kept the style alive and it is still practised today.

§

The Bok Hok Pai Test of Courage

II

Eight students waited in the long dark corridor as the old monk fumbled with the rusty lock on a huge oak door. As the door eventually creaked open the student monks walked in silently in single file to await the coming of their master, the leader of the bok hok pai system of kung fu.

The system of bok hok pai, or White Crane, was devised by the Tibetan lamas. It was a very ancient system of fighting that involved many complicated movements, and was only ever studied by the best of the best from the other styles of kung fu. Legend relates that a lama was meditating on a hillside when he was disturbed by a great commotion. Looking up, he saw a terrific fight in progress between a white crane and a mountain ape. The ape would charge at the crane, but the wily bird evaded the charges and retaliated with its wings and claws. After a heated battle the ape turned and fled, blinded in one eye. The lama created eight different techniques based upon what he had witnessed. These used the natural movements of the white crane and incorporated the ape's footwork and grabbing manoeuvres.

For the next hundred years the system was further developed using the lamas' knowledge of medicine and the vital points of the body. Special breathing techniques were introduced based upon the lamas' experience of living at such high altitudes in the Himalayas and breathing the rarefied air at the roof of the world. The advanced techniques of these breathing methods were said to give added strength in combat, prolong longevity and enable eighty-year-old men to fight like men in the midst of youth.

Originally, the system was reserved solely for use by the elite bodyguards of the emperors of China. Bok hok pai fighters were chosen to be the imperial bodyguards not only because they were the most formidable of all fighters but also because they could be trusted to die defending the emperor. Known by only a select few, the system was kept a closely guarded secret for many centuries. Most of the masters of the Chinese kung fu schools never dreamed that there was a Shaolin-type fighting monastery high in the mountains of Tibet. Its students were selected every three years by a special process of elimination based upon expertise, and then escorted by a lama into Tibet. For the last two hundred miles of the journey, the students were blindfolded and roped together so that they would not slip on the dangerous mountain paths.

As the eight students waited in the gloom of a huge half-lit hall they each knew that the final stage of their training was about to commence – the dreaded Cotton Needle Set. This was a set pattern of fighting movements that they had to perform in front of the headmaster. The Cotton Needle Set was not new to them; as young students they had practised it over and over again, but this time it would be different. In training the set would be carried out balanced on poles that were about a foot (30 cm) high. However, today the students would have to attempt the advanced mui fa joong ('plum blossom poles'), where the Cotton Needle Set is performed balanced on poles that are 10 feet long (3 metres) and only 6 inches (15 cm) in diameter, buried in the ground to a depth of 3 feet (90 cm). There were fourteen of these poles arranged in the shape of plum blossom petals.

A shuffling sound was heard and in walked the slightly built headmaster, followed by a dozen monks. The headmaster explained that all they had to do was climb up the poles and execute their Cotton Needle Set, just like they had done so many times before. He explained that they should disregard anything around them no matter what. 'Concentrate, perform and lose yourself within the set.' He went on to say, 'The true kung fu man concentrates only upon the task at hand, your training will bring you through. Do not let dark imaginings nor fear enter into your mind. If you do, you are finished!'

By now the other monks had lit candles and the hall was bathed in a glimmering light. The students turned around to face their ordeal and what they saw froze them to the bone. In front of them were the usual fourteen poles but instead of being a foot high they were some seven feet high. In between the poles were hundreds of wicked-looking, sharpened bamboo stakes. Some short, some long but all capable of killing a man should he fall from his pole.

The students went to climb the poles, but only seconds later a scream was heard as the lead student fell to his death upon the spikes. Because he had rushed up the pole in an attempt to be first to the top, he was the first to discover the beeswax that covered the last part of the pole. This deadly lesson taught the others to expect the unexpected – a valuable trait in a bodyguard. They reached the top of the poles and began to go through the set. Screams were heard as two more students fell to their deaths. Their fear of the sharpened bamboo stakes had been too much to overcome. Instead of concentrating on the set, which they had done thousands of times before, they allowed their thoughts to be clouded by the fact that they were precariously perched high above lethal stakes.

The test over, the remaining students climbed down the poles ready to take their place as the elite bodyguard of the emperor of China. The heavy oak door was closed until the next time.

§

The Death Touch

II

No one can engage in the activities of the martial arts for too long without coming into contact with, or hearing about, a mysterious energy called chi. In karate and aikido it is known as ki, and yogis refer to it as prana. This powerful unseen force lies within everyone and is capable of being tapped at any given moment by those who know how. The user can summon up abnormal amounts of strength and apply it instantly.

Chi energy is cultivated in virtually every kung fu style practised today. To the ancient Chinese it was the very substance that the universe was made of. The concept of a vital life energy permeated through the martial arts and into the realms of medicine, for example in the healing skills of acupuncture and acupressure. As with everything Chinese the fundamental interplay of yin and yang is involved: what is good can also be evil. The good side of chi is that it can cure; the dark side that it can kill. The use of chi to kill is known as dim mak, or the 'death touch'.

There is a legend that a doctor at the imperial court, who was skilled in acupuncture, accidentally killed a nephew of one of the emperor's concubines. Although not important in the royal hierarchy he was nevertheless a nephew. The emperor was outraged and wanted the doctor beheaded, but then decided that he should spend the rest of his life in prison to contemplate upon what he had done to a member of the royal house.

The dungeon within the Forbidden City (the home of the emperors) was damp and very confined. The doctor, who was also a kung fu master of the Iron Palm style, resigned himself to a lifetime in these surroundings. Each day he would meditate and then to cultivate his chi he would systematically go through all his special breathing exercises.

About two years into his sentence he was sent for by the emperor. The favourite concubine of the emperor was having fits of coughing and the doctor's replacement could not cure her. As the doctor entered the room of the concubine the people gathered around the bedside could not believe his appearance. Although now in rags his face positively radiated a healthy glow and the rest of his body looked toned and in the peak of condition. Walking to the bedside, he pulled out his acupuncture needles and inserted them at points all over the woman's body. It was then that he realised that the women was the concubine whose son he had accidentally killed. She too recognised him and screamed for him to be taken away, so the doctor was escorted back to his cell.

Three days later, and now in a panic, the emperor again ordered the doctor to be brought from his cell. The concubine was still ill and had sunk into a deep sleep from which she could not be wakened. The doctor treated the woman and within a few days she was awake and as fit and healthy as ever. The emperor was overjoyed and announced that he would pardon the doctor. Unknown to the emperor, however, the concubine arranged for another prisoner to be freed instead of the doctor. The jailer informed the doctor of what had happened but could do nothing.

A few years passed, then one day the jailer rushed in and told the doctor that the whole of the kingdom was in an uproar as the heir to the throne had fallen from his horse and lapsed into a coma. None of the doctors in the city could wake him and so the kingdom was being searched in an attempt to find the doctor. As dusk fell a noise was heard and the concubine appeared at the doctor's cell door. She begged him to help as the heir concerned was her eldest son. The doctor asked, 'How do I know that after I help your son you won't put me back in this cell?' The concubine promised she wouldn't, but the doctor knew only too well that she could not be trusted. So, pretending to believe her, he went to the bedside of the prince and once again administered his acupuncture treatment. The next day, to everyone's joy, the boy awoke and fully recovered. The doctor rubbed his hands together as though overjoyed, but really he was conjuring up massive amounts of chi energy from within his body. He stood up and placed his open palm in a fatherly fashion upon the concubine's shoulder and pressed lightly, saying to the woman that to ensure the recovery would be permanent the boy needed a special broth made from secret herbs and so he would need to leave the city for a day to gather them.

The concubine not to be outwitted said she would send her two other sons with him as an escort. The three left the city and headed for the mountains. Once he had found the herbs the doctor thanked the concubine's sons for escorting him and shook hands with them in a strange fashion. But all they felt was a kind of warmth emanate from his hand. They then accompanied him back to the city. Halfway there both sons, within seconds of each other, fell from their horses dead. The doctor simply rode off into the night and was never heard off again.

At the palace the next day the recovered prince grew sick again and without the doctor's care was dead by the morning. The concubine was quite beside herself, then she too collapsed as though she had had a stroke and was dead within minutes. In one swoop the doctor had exacted his revenge by using the art of the Death Touch, dim mak. He had known that if their mother was a person whose word was not to be trusted, then surely her offspring would be made of similar mettle. So not only was he avenged but the kingdom was saved from a potential tyrant and his family.

§

The Drunken Boxer

II

There are many different styles of kung fu in China and their origins are lost in the mists of time. One style in particular, that of tsui pa hsien, is both unique and intriguing. It is known as 'drunken man boxing' and is vastly different from the monkey system drunken style. Tsui pa hsien uses as one of its vital elements a method of concealing a fighter's ability by adopting the attitude of being intoxicated. Many of the techniques in drunken kung fu can be extremely devastating against an unsuspecting opponent. Perhaps more than any other style this one places extreme emphasis upon fluidity of movement.

Many years ago in a village in southern China there was a kung fu man of mediocre talent. What he lacked in expertise he made up for in bragging. He and his friends would regularly finish training and then head straight for the local tavern where they would consume copious amounts of liquor. One day a travelling pot-seller arrived in the village who was also a master in the Black Tiger system of kung fu and something of a champion fighter in his own right. After completing his business he retired for the evening to the local inn for a quiet meal. A gang of rowdy youths, including the kung fu man of mediocre talent, entered the tavern, laughing and shouting. About an hour later an argument erupted amongst them as to who was the best fighter at their kung fu school. They then began to throw beer about and generally make a nuisance of themselves. The innkeeper was too afraid to say anything, so he just put up with the noise. The Black Tiger master, how-ever, could not stand the shouting any longer, so he stood up and challenged their best fighter to a match the next day. The kung fu man with the mediocre talent was the first to accept the challenge and promptly fell to the floor dead drunk.

The next day, still only half-sober, the mediocre fighter was met by his friends who had been finding out about the challenger. One said, 'He is a Black Tiger exponent, and a master, not a student like us.' Another explained, 'He has been training for over twenty years and they say he has never been beaten.' Upon hearing this the mediocre fighter became very apprehensive. This time, he thought, his mouth had really got him into a lot of trouble. He said to his friends that as they still had about two hours or so before the fight it may be a good idea to go to the inn for a drink, to which they all agreed. The fighter thought that the alcohol would perhaps give him some much needed courage.

In order to try to calm his nerves the young fighter drank a considerable amount of alcohol, much more than he had intended. The time of the fight arrived and his friends walked with the now staggering fighter to meet the master of the Black Tiger. With all his inhibitions removed by the alcohol, the young fighter actually engaged his opponent in a very cocky manner. An interesting situation developed. The young boxer, who up to then had always been stiff and awkward in the kung fu class, especially when executing techniques, suddenly became elusive and fluid in his movements. The master really had to work hard to try and hit him. As the fight wore on the master found the young fighter an impossible target. The drunken youth when attacked just lashed out with anything that came to mind, but the speed of his hands was quite incredible. The youth answered each attempted blow from the master with a barrage of offensive techniques that seemed to come from virtually every direction.

The older, much more experienced master began to think that he had been tricked into the fight, because the young man was almost unreachable, and his strikes were being parried as though all his years of experience counted for nothing. Unfortunately for the master, the young fighter's mouth was going as fast as his blows. The master began to feel uncomfortable. 'Surely', he thought, 'anyone this confident has plans to do more than beat me in a fight. Maybe the youth wants to kill me.' This unsettled the master so much that he called a halt to the fight, announcing the youth the winner. He then asked if he could become a student and learn this fascinating and devastating style. The youth, who by now was beginning to sober up, realised that he had had a lucky escape. But instead of retiring to the inn with everyone else he took the master back to his house and explained everything. With the master's expertise of kung fu moves and the youth's input, the two eventually came up with the drunken man system of kung fu.

The Teamaster
and
the Samurai

∏

The art of making tea to the Japanese is deeply ritualistic and involves profound Zen qualities. It is almost a religious ceremony. Therefore a master of the tea is held in the same high regard as a martial arts master.

About three centuries ago, in medieval Japan, a teamaster was walking through the busy streets of Kyoto on his way to perform the O-Cha-no (tea ceremony) when he accidentally brushed up against a samurai. In doing so he touched one of the samurai's swords with the back of his hand. The samurai was greatly offended and immediately demanded a duel to make amends for the insult. (For to a samurai his sword was his soul and to touch it was the equivalent of slapping him in the face.) The teamaster offered his apologies but to no avail and the samurai said that he would meet him the next day at dawn at the city gates. The teamaster was greatly disturbed about the impending duel, after all, what did he know about fighting? Arriving at his destination, he explained to his host, who had hired him to teach his daughter the tea ceremony, all about the incident. His host said that unfortunately the samurai he had inadvertently insulted was a great fighter who had never lost a fight.

After giving the merchant's daughter her lesson, the teamaster hurried to see his close friend the swordmaker to ask if he could borrow a sword.

The swordmaker asked, 'What are you going to do with the sword? You don't know how to fight, you've been a master of the tea all your life. To give you a sword would be useless.'

'So what should I do?' retorted the teamaster, 'I have to go and meet the samurai, honour demands it.'

'Then go!' replied his friend. 'You can't fight, so meet your end with honour and as a last gesture of your time here on earth perform the ceremony of the tea.'

At dawn the next day the samurai was pacing up and down outside the city gates, waiting for his opponent. Several inquisitive passers-by had stopped to see what was transpiring. Then in the distance the samurai saw the teamaster approaching. 'Before we fight', the teamaster said, 'I will perform the ceremony of the tea.' And with that he knelt down and began to unfold a lined holder and prepared to make the tea. He deftly started a small fire and brewed the water, then with great care he sprinkled some powdered tea into the now boiling water. Grasping the brush he whisked the tea, first in a clockwise then in an anticlockwise motion. The samurai could not believe what was going on. In all of his duels he had never faced an opponent so calm in the face of death.

After about half an hour of this ritual, the samurai strode over to the teamaster and threw him on the ground, saying, 'Teamaster, of all the men I have killed many have begged forgiveness before I decapitated them. Some offered me gold to spare their lives. Some screamed and shouted and tried to run away before I killed them. But never have I seen bravery such as yours. You face certain death and yet you make tea. The tea is not rushed, nor the ceremony compromised. Truly, you are not only a great teamaster but a man who does not fear death. I wonder if I could face death with such calm. Please, teamaster, forgive my challenge and take me as your student in the tea ceremony, so that I too may learn how to face death with such calm and repose as you have displayed here today.' The teamaster looked up, smiled and nodded his assent.

The
Chi Gung
Breath of Life

II

The art of chi gung is essential if one is to acquire the inner power needed to progress in the martial arts, and also to develop the techniques that sometimes go beyond fighting. Both the Chinese and Japanese believe that chi is the very stuff of the universe and that chi breathing exercises connect us to it.

In China a long time ago most wandering priests were also kung fu masters, and it was they who carried the news of recent happenings from one village to another. One day a master of the White Eyebrow system was hurrying along a country road carrying an important message to the mayor of a big town some fifty miles away. The message concerned an invading force that was wreaking havoc amongst the villages in a neighbouring region. The information he was carrying would allow the people of the town enough time to prepare their defences and so hopefully vanquish the invaders.

As he rounded a bend in the road he came upon a small village. As he got nearer he saw that it had been ransacked and dead bodies lay all about. It was obvious the marauders had been there and burnt the place down, killing all the people. As he walked quickly past the devastation he heard the sound of a child crying. Turning he saw a five-year-old boy sitting outside the remains of a burnt-out hut. The bodies of a man and a woman were lying near by, obviously the boy's parents. About fifteen yards away were two large dogs intent upon having the child as a meal.

The kung fu master did not know what to do. He shooed the dogs away but then was faced with the problem of what to do with the boy. He could not leave him for the dogs to eat and yet, because of his urgent errand, could not take the boy with him. He therefore thought that at least he could put him out of harm's way. So he picked the boy up and carried him to the village well, then lowered him down in the bucket. At the bottom of the well was a huge stone protruding from the water and the boy climbed out of the bucket and on to the stone. The priest then went on his way. At least, he thought, the wild animals will not get him and tear him limb from limb. The boy will just die a serene death of exhaustion and starvation. Although not a pleasant thought, it was the lesser of the two evils.

Some months later, having saved the day with his message and the invading marauders having been soundly beaten, the priest was heading back down the road that passed through the village where he had found the boy. He stopped by the well with the intention of retrieving the boy's remains and giving him a decent burial. As he approached he heard a sound echoing up from within, looking down he was amazed to see the young boy still sitting upon the protruding stone looking quite fit and healthy. 'How could this be?' thought the priest. 'With no food he should have been dead weeks ago.' Then he heard the sound of a croak, just like that of a frog. Looking through the gloom of the well the kung fu priest saw that it was the boy who was making the noise, as one croak followed another. The lad was behaving just like a frog. The priest told the boy to get in the bucket and he hauled him up out of the well.

As the bucket came to the top the boy let out another huge croaking sound. It was then that the priest realised the boy had survived by drinking the water in the well and copying the frog' s breathing method – taking huge gulps of air and sinking it deep into his abdomen. The air, the elixir of life, combined with the water had kept him alive for all those months. The priest pulled the boy out of the bucket and took him home with him. In the years that followed, the priest, charted the boy's every breathing method and eventually formulated a chi gung breathing system that complemented his own system of kung fu.

§

The Death of a Legend

II

No book dealing with anything relating to the martial arts would be complete without mention of a man who some regarded as a living legend. That man is the late Bruce Lee. Even today people still feel his death is surrounded by curious circumstances. Not so, he died an untimely death but the facts surrounding his death were duly noted and recorded by the British Home Office. The account of the events leading up to his death are as follows.

The film company Warner Brothers offered Bruce Lee the starring role in a forthcoming movie called *Blood and Steel*, later retitled *Enter the Dragon*, which co-starred American actor John Saxon. The critics said it was nothing more than a second-rate 'Bond' film, yet audiences packed cinemas worldwide to see what is now regarded as the best example of the genre.

Martial artists and martial arts actors were signed up to give the movie an authentic flavour of realism rather than using trained stunt men. Bruce Lee used a variety of classical Chinese weapons in the film, including the now infamous nunchaku (rice flail). It would be an understatement to say that Bruce Lee was very satisfied with the film and expected it to be his biggest to date. Unfortunately, he never saw its success.

Whilst *Enter the Dragon* was awaiting release, Bruce resumed work on an earlier film he had left called *Game of Death*. On 10th May 1973, whilst dubbing the sound and dialogue for *Enter the Dragon*, he collapsed. By the time Lee was rushed to hospital he was having difficulty breathing. The doctors fought to save his life and, though it was touch and go, finally succeeded. They considered various possible causes, such as overwork or kidney malfunction, but the most likely was a cerebral oedema, a swelling of the fluid which surrounds the brain. When Lee was well again he had a complete check-up by the best doctors in America, who could find nothing wrong with him. In fact they told the thirty-two-year-old star that he had the body of an eighteen-year-old!

On 20th July Bruce Lee went with producer Raymond Chow to visit the home of actress and friend

Betty Ting Pei to discuss a part for her in the unfin-
ished *Game of Death*. Lee complained of a headache
and went to lie down. Chow agreed to meet him
later at a restaurant, where they were to have talks
with Bond star George Lazenby over a major role in
the same film. But when Betty went to wake Lee
some time later she could not get any response. She
telephoned for Chow to come round and when he
too was unable to stir Lee, he called a doctor. An
ambulance rushed Lee to hospital where this time
doctors could not revive him. The 'fittest man in the
world' was dead.

There have been many theories explaining Lee's
death, which include: suicide with a gun; drug over-
dose; being killed by jealous kung fu masters; or by
an expert in the secret art of dim mak, the delayed
death touch. It has been suggested that he had accidentally invoked ill luck and evil spirits in using the
word 'death' in his films – the Chinese are a very
superstitious people. It was further suggested that
Bruce Lee had gone into hiding to escape the Triads.

The official autopsy, carried out by the British
Home Office, because Hong Kong was at the time a
British Crown Protectorate, revealed that his brain
had swollen like a sponge and weighed 1,575 grams
instead of the normal 1,400 grams. Another coroner,
specially sent out to Hong Kong to carry out an

independent report, such was the importance of Lee's death, confirmed the finding: death from a brain oedema caused by hypersensitivity to one of the two compounds in the Equagesic tablet Betty Ting Pei had given him for his headache. The coroner's verdict was death by misadventure.

His body was transported to America and buried in Lake View Cemetery, just off 15th Avenue East in Seattle. The graveside rests on a hill that overlooks nearby Lake Washington. There the 'little dragon' (Bruce Lee's nickname), the founder of jeet kune do, ('way of the intercepting fist') aged only thirty-three, sleeps for ever.

§

Beaten by a Novice

Π

In a small village just outside the city of Nagasaki in Japan, there lived a karate master of the shotokan style. He earned his living by teaching karate to the men and boys of the village and also as a bone-setter. Many karate masters were adept at bone-setting and herbal medicine. His students were loyal and disciplined, and diligently practised their techniques day after day in search of mastery of the art.

One particular student showed extreme prowess as a fighter and was always chosen by the master to represent the school at tournaments. These usually occurred at special times in the year to celebrate either a particular season or the birthday of a god. The student's name was Kiro and it was expected that when the master retired he would, as the head student, take over the teaching at the school.

Kiro was liked by all the students because he took time out from his own training to help those who were struggling with some of the more complicated movements. As time passed Kiro's reputation in the region grew and grew.

One day his master entered him into a tournament in a town some miles away. It was the Festival of the August Moon and so everyone was celebrating and, of course, a karate tournament always got the people excited. Kiro faced various opponents throughout the day and as he beat them his confidence grew. With still a long way to go before the final, he was faced with a short, lean long-haired fighter whom Kiro remembered used to live in his village. Kiro knew he could win easily as his skill was far superior, and he did indeed win the bout and went on to win the tournament as well. Afterwards there was much celebrating and Kiro's master was overjoyed that his top student had yet again won the day.

Later that night, as Kiro was enjoying a celebratory dinner with his master, there was a great commotion in the street. Rushing outside, Kiro saw the long-haired fighter running his way with a small piglet under his arm and about twenty villagers chasing him. 'Stop thief! Stop thief!' shouted the villagers in hot pursuit. Kiro suddenly stepped out in front of the thief and told him to drop the pig and give himself up. The thief lashed out with a front kick which Kiro saw coming and blocked. Without dropping the pig, the thief turned half to the side and released a side kick that sent Kiro spinning backwards and on to the ground. The long-haired youth then made good his escape. By now Kiro's master had come out and had witnessed the encounter.

'Master, how is it that I was beaten by a fighter that I have only recently beaten, and he was running barely with any breath left with a pig under his arm as well?' asked Kiro.

'Kiro,' the master replied, 'do not doubt your talent as a fighter. Instead let me tell you a Zen parable that will perhaps explain to you what you have just experienced.'

The master then went on to relate the story of the fox chasing a rabbit.

'A Zen master was out walking with his student. The student saw the fox chasing a rabbit and said to his master, "I wonder which one will win?" "According to an old fable," his master replied, "the rabbit will get away from the fox." "Surely not, the fox is faster." "But the rabbit will still escape," insisted the Zen master. "Why are you so certain?" asked the student. "Because the fox is running for his dinner but the rabbit is running for his life." '

Kiro at once understood the meaning of the parable and the reason why he had been unable to stop the long-haired thief.

§

King
of the
Thai Boxers

Π

The old kingdom of Siam, as Thailand was once known, lies on the Southeast Asian peninsula, bordered by Burma, Laos and Cambodia. This proud country has fiercely protected her borders and resisted all attempts at conquest. It was able to do so because of the amazing fighting spirit of its people, and the many heroes who have appeared throughout Siam's turbulent history. Of all these heroes perhaps none was more braver or more loved by the people than Nai Khanom Dtom.

From an early age Nai Khanom Dtom displayed brilliant fighting skills in the national sport of muay Thai (Thai boxing). As he grew into manhood many fighters challenged him but he overcame them all to eventually gain the title of the best fighter in all Siam. Apart from his boxing skills, Nai was also a brilliant athlete and a courageous man. It was always Nai who led the first battle charges during the many wars Siam had with Burma, and he was always in the thickest part of the hand-to-hand fighting, yet he was never wounded. Siam's enemies began to think that he was not a mortal at all but had been sent by the gods.

As the legends grew, the king of Burma saw that the very name of Nai Khanom Dtom was affecting the morale of his troops. He therefore devised a plan to catch the great fighter and prove to his army that this Siamese hero was mortal just like them. He picked two hundred of his finest troops from his personal bodyguard and armed half of them with elephant spears. These were normally used for fighting from the backs of elephants and so were three feet longer than normal spears. The other hundred men would be armed with snaring nets, which would be used to ensure Nai Khanom Dtom's capture. The two hundred soldiers were not to engage the enemy with the rest of the army. Their only aim was to move in on Nai Khanom Dtom and attack him together. No man, the king thought, could fight two hundred men armed to the teeth and win!

During their next incursion into Siam, the Burmese as usual faced Nai Khanom Dtom at the forefront of the Siamese army. However, despite a fearsome fight the two hundred soldiers managed to take Nai prisoner and brought him before the king of Burma. To prove that he was nothing more than just a lucky fighter and not sent by the gods, the king staged a huge boxing tournament in which Nai had to face twelve of Burma's champion bando fighters (the Burmese martial art, similar to muay Thai). The king laughingly said that if Nai could beat all twelve he would go free, believing that it would take a superhuman fighter to even get past the first two.

So the next day in a stadium packed with thousands of people all baying for Nai Khanom Dtom's blood, the great tournament began. Each one of the Burmese champions wanted to be the one that vanquished the great Siamese hero and so become heroes themselves. But as each fighter went against Nai they each met a swift death from lightning elbow strikes or murderous knee blows. Almost invisible kicks seemed to come from nowhere and suddenly connect with bone-crunching accuracy and another so-called champion would drop dead to the ground.

As the day wore on into early evening, Nai had slain nine of his adversaries. The spectators, who earlier had been cheering for their champions, suddenly began to cheer for this magnificent fighter from Siam. They were full of admiration for the prisoner who had fought and killed nine men without rest for almost eight hours and was not even wounded. By the end of the day twelve bodies lay on the ground of the dusty stadium, and standing tall and undefeated was the great Nai Khanom Dtom. The entire crowd stood chanting his name. The king of Burma had no alternative but to let him go free.

Today, many centuries after that event, Thai boxers honour Nai Khanom Dtom by dedicating one fight night each year to his memory.

§

The Flower
of
Youth

II

In ancient times the present-day country of Korea
was divided into three kingdoms: Silla, Paekche
and Koguryu. Koguryu was the largest of the three
and occupied the entire territory of what is now
Manchuria, plus part of the Korean peninsula. This
kingdom later became known as Koryo, from which
the modern name of Korea is derived.

About a thousand years ago Koguryu attempted
to invade and conquer the two smaller kingdoms.
Paekche was attacked first and was defeated. In Silla,
following what had happened to its neighbour, an
edict was issued that every able-bodied person was to
train in military arts. The object, in effect, was to turn
the kingdom into a nation of fighters.

The very best of the best fighters were then taken
to the capital to be inducted into a newly formed

special force called the Hwarang ('the flower of manhood'). From within this force would come the future generals and leaders of the kingdom. Instrumental in the organisation was a much revered fighting monk named Won Kwang Bopsa. Even the king of Silla sent his sons and best soldiers to his temple-like school to be trained. From this nucleus emerged huge armies of highly trained specialist soldiers, expert in all the known martial arts and proficient in the handling of every weapon imaginable. It was a kind of thinking-man's military academy, where under the guidance of Won Kwang Bopsa each person learnt a moral as well as a military code. Philosophy and fighting were taught hand in hand. Because of this ingenious system, Silla eventually became the leading force and triumphed over its enemies, although there were many battles and great feats of heroism before this was accomplished.

On one occasion the Hwarang was faced with an army ten times its size. A young warrior, barely sixteen, in the flower of youth, and only recently qualified as a member of the Hwarang, rode out from the ranks. His name was Kwan Chang and he was the son of the famous general Pumil. His father watched proudly as he trotted to the front in order to lead his detachment into battle. Drawing his sword he charged the enemy. The battle proved to be hard and long, but the vastly outnumbered Hwarang fought well and slew huge numbers of the enemy. In the midst of all this carnage, Chang was captured but not before he had slain fifteen of the enemy.

He was brought before the enemy leader and his helmet was pulled from his head. His captors were shocked to see that the warrior who had fought so bravely was only a mere boy hardly into puberty. He was also recognised as the great general's son. Praising him for his bravery, the enemy leader felt compassion for the boy as he had a son of a similar age. So, rather than execute him he allowed Chang to return to the Hwarang. The enemy leader commented to one of his commanders, 'If this is the face of our enemy, a sixteen-year-old boy with bravery I have never seen before, then what hope has our army when their men attack.'

Kwan Chang returned to his own forces, asked for a sip of water and then sought permission to ride out again at the head of another detachment. Within minutes he was once more right in the thick of things. Fighting his way forward into the enemy's deepest lines, he met and slew the enemy leader's second in command. In doing so he was again captured, but this time there was no mercy for the boy. The enemy leader said, 'I spared you your life once because of your youth, but now you return and take the life of my best field commander. For this you will die.' The boy was taken away and beheaded. His bravery was not forgotten, however, and the memory of it was a further inspiration to the Hwarang in ridding their country of the invaders.

The Journey of 1000 Miles Begins First in the Mind

∏

There was once a youth who had studied karate for nearly five years. He would learn all the techniques as fast as he could and then beg his master to assess him in order that he could go up a grade. This went on year after year and all the time the youth was continually pressing his teacher to test him so that he could rise to a higher rank. In the end his master said, 'I can teach you nothing more about karate. To take yourself further you must seek guidance from one that is better than I. He is my old sensei (teacher) and lives very far from here.'

The youth rushed off to the dojo (training place) of his master's master. After travelling across Japan for nearly a month he finally came upon the martial arts school of his master's sensei. However, it was closed and upon enquiring from some karate students training near by he found out that the sensei had gone to visit a local shrine to lay offerings, and would not be back until the next day. The youth entered into discussion with the students and before too long he was telling them what grade he was and how he wanted to train with their sensei in order to hurry through the grades to become a master himself. The students quickly tired of his conversation and left, so the youth bedded down for the night under the porch of the karate school.

The next morning he saw the sensei approaching. He stood back as the teacher opened the door of the dojo and then followed him in. Upon seeing the youth the sensei asked what he wanted from him.

'I wish to become a student at your school and be the finest karateka ('one who practises karate') in Japan,' the youth replied. 'How long must I train to accomplish this?' he asked.

'Ten years at least,' the sensei answered.

'Ten years is a long time,' said the youth. 'What if I studied twice as hard as all your other students, how long then?'

'Twenty years.'

'Twenty years! What if I practise night and day and cut my sleeping time by half?'

'Thirty years.'

'Why is it that each time I say I will work harder

you tell me that it will take longer? It doesn't make sense.'

The old sensei smiled at the youth and replied, 'The answer is clear. When one eye is fixed upon your destination, there is only one eye left with which to find the way.'

§

The Secret Champion

II

Centuries ago a Mongolian emperor and his great armies were encamped on the borders of a small Asian kingdom. He had sent out spies weeks before to get information about the people, the royal house and the strengths and weakness of the country. On their return the spies informed him that the terrain of the country was treacherous and would cause a great loss of men and animals, and as they moved through the mountain ranges they would become easy prey for guerrilla-type attacks. They also reported that the people's love of their king was so great that they would fight to the death before either their king or their land was taken.

The Mongolian emperor upon hearing this thought that perhaps guile would be better than an outright attack. So he hatched a plan that he thought would succeed without the need for any fighting at all. He knew that the king of this country was a fervent martial arts devotee, like himself, and could be approached in a civil manner because he was a reasonable man. He therefore arranged a meeting with the king to put a proposition to him.

At first the Mongol emperor said that because his army was so huge it would be only a matter of time before he destroyed the king's forces. In doing so, however, both sides would suffer great loss of life. He then explained that because his army was so large and the king's country so small, the king would lose at least half his population. Upon hearing this the king offered to pay the Mongol a yearly tribute of cattle and produce from every village, providing that no Mongol soldiers stepped foot in the kingdom. This seemed reasonable, but the emperor knew in his heart that he wanted the kingdom.

'I know', he said, 'you are a martial arts devotee as I am myself. What say you, we pick the best fighter from each side, they fight to the death and the winner takes everything. If my fighter wins, we take your kingdom without a battle. If your man defeats my Chinese champion, then you have my word and solemn promise we will leave your land for ever.'

The king tried to think of a way out, but seeing none he reluctantly agreed to the duel of champions.

The emperor went away smirking, knowing that no one in the whole of Asia had a hope of beating his champion. The Chinese fighter had killed more than sixty-five men in fights that never lasted more than five minutes. He felt certain that the kingdom would soon be his.

Two days later the fighters met at the arranged time and place. A vast crowd had come to see this great fight of the champions. The giant Chinese fighter looked across at his opponent who was dressed in a kind of hooded cloak which obscured his face. A gong sounded for the fight to commence and the cloaked fighter discarded his robe. A great gasp came from the crowd and an even bigger gasp from the Mongol emperor, because the champion of the small kingdom was none other than the king himself, who was sometimes known as the Tiger King. Even the Chinese fighter looked a little taken back, knowing that he had to fight and kill a king.

In a flash, before anyone realised what was happening, the king had leapt into the air and executed a flying kick that took the eyes out of the head of the Chinese fighter. Upon landing a few feet away from his now blinded adversary, he leapt into the air again and unleashed another flying kick. This time the heel of his foot struck his opponent's temple with a sickening crunch and the Chinese champion fell dead.

The Mongol emperor was aghast because his great champion had been killed by the king of the country he had wished to conquer. It was a great loss of face. He bowed to the king with humility and true to his word gathered his army and left the borders of the kingdom never to return. The people rejoiced that their king, Pra Chao Sua, had saved their beloved country of Siam.

A Lesson
in
Humility

Π

There was a young man who had been studying Eagle Claw kung fu for three years and was now reasonably adept. Unfortunately, he would use his skill to terrorise the people of a nearby village. Every week he would go to the village and bully and push people around. Sometimes he would just hit them for no reason, or he would take things without paying and, of course, beat them up if they tried to stop him.

One afternoon whilst making his rounds of the town's taverns, and slapping anyone who happened to get in his way, he careered into an old man who was slowly walking down the street. The old man stumbled but quickly regained his balance and managed not to fall over. Any other person would have apologised at once, but the youth just sneered at him.

'Watch where you are going you old fool. You

obviously don't know who I am otherwise you would have been more careful not to bump into me.'

The old man looked up at the youth and in a croaky voice said, 'Don't you respect your elders? I did when I was your age. You're nothing more than a bully.'

The youth was enraged that an old man should have the temerity to talk to him in such a way. He began to hurl insults and abuse at him and then threatened him with a good hiding. The old man was still standing in the bully's path, who then screamed at him to get out of the way. But the old man did not move and this made the youth even angrier.

'You either move or I will beat you to the ground for annoying me so much. Look around you, nobody is going to step in and help you.'

The old man briefly scanned the gathering crowd and saw the look of fear upon their faces. At least, he thought, the boy was right about that assumption. The next minute the youth pounced on the old man, knocking him to the ground with his fists. Once on the ground he began to kick him, then he moved in close with the intention of dropping both his knees into the old man's stomach. However, the old man pushed out his hand and caught the youth on his chest, over his heart. It could hardly be described as a blow, but for the moment the youth stopped his attack because he was laughing uncontrollably.

'What was that old man?' he asked mockingly, 'Did you hit me with a feather or was it an attempt at a punch? You barely ruffled my tunic.'

The bully then turned and left, laughing all the way up the street and into the nearest tavern. The crowd that had witnessed the incident went over to the old man to offer aid. But the old man jumped sprightly to his feet and standing erect walked briskly off in the direction of his home.

About two weeks later the bullying youth began to feel horrible pains in his chest. Over the following few days his sleep was erratic and every time he had a meal he was violently sick afterwards. He began to feel weak all the time and only felt like sleeping, but when he tried to sleep he could not. In a little over a month he had lost twenty pounds in weight and was beginning to look remarkably scrawny. He had not trained in his kung fu for nearly two months. It was only after two months that it dawned on him that in some way the old man's feather-like blow had done this to him. He also knew that he was going to die, so in a fit of remorse he asked his brother to seek out the old man and beg his forgiveness for the way he had treated him. When the brother knocked upon the old man's door he felt as though the old man had been expecting him.

'My brother begs your forgiveness sir,' said the youth. 'He is so very sorry for what happened.'

'I thought he might be', said the old man. 'Where is he now?'

The brother replied, 'He is at home dying sir, but he wanted me to apologise on his behalf before he goes.'

Upon hearing this, the old man went with the brother to see the bullying youth at his home. His agonised cries could be heard from the street. Entering the house and seeing the youth in such pain, the old man listened as the boy professed in short, staggered breaths how sorry he was for everything. The old man believed that he had learned his lesson. He then pulled a bottle of dark green liquid from under his tunic and gave the boy two doses of the medicine.

Turning to the brother he said, 'Give him this liquid twice a day and he will soon get better.'

Within the week the boy was back on his feet and getting stronger every day. After two weeks he went to see the old man to thank him, and to tell him how he would change his ways. The old man told him that he was in fact a kung fu teacher and an expert in dim mak – the art of the death touch. He went on to say that the villagers had sent for him some weeks ago because of the youth's bullying. The boy dropped to his knees and begged the teacher to take him on as a personal student, which the old man did and the youth eventually became his best student.

§

Look Beyond the Target

Π

Lu Sei was an archer of great skill and accuracy, and he was known far and wide. He won all the local archery competitions and such was his fame that he opened an archery school to teach students kyudo ('the way of the bow'). Over the next few years he taught many students and became reasonably wealthy.

One day a beggar came to town, asking for alms. He observed Lu Sei conducting an archery training session with his top students. He stopped and sat down on the grass to watch. The beggar noticed that every time Lu Sei came to shoot he never missed, each arrow found its way right into the centre of the target. After about an hour of this the beggar walked over to Lu Sei and congratulated him upon his fine marksmanship. He asked him where he had learned to shoot a bow with such brilliance. Lu Sei replied that he had been practising archery ever since he could walk, and over the years had got better and better. As a teenager he had entered competitions and won them all.

'But surely at some stage you must have had a master to teach you the finer elements of kyudo?' the beggar asked.

'Oh no,' replied Lu Sei, 'I taught myself everything. I did not need a master. What could a master have taught me that I don't already know?'

'There is more to shooting the bow than just hitting the target time after time. Have you ever shot at anyone in anger?' asked the beggar.

'No, never,' replied Lu Sei.

'Then how do you know you could defend yourself with your art in a battle?'

'I could quite easily do that,' retorted Lu Sei. 'Or had you not noticed that I never miss what I aim at. With my accuracy, I would probably be the finest archer in the army.'

The beggar smiled, 'I think it is you who forgets that a target does not fire back at you. If your only experience of archery is that of firing for your ego's sake, then I think you still have a lot to learn about the true art of kyudo.'

Lu Sei was now beginning to get a little annoyed

with the dirty beggar who had just walked into his class and tried to tell him, the great Lu Sei, about kyudo.

He turned to the beggar and said, 'If you have so much to say about the way of the bow, maybe you would like to show me what you can do?'

Lu Sei handed the beggar the bow and one arrow, while the students looked on with interest. The beggar lifted the bow and fired the arrow. It hit the target but was just a little off centre. Lu Sei snatched the bow off the beggar, quickly aimed and almost without any effort fired an arrow into the dead centre of the target.

Smirking, he turned to the beggar and said, 'Interesting, you know so much about kyudo and yet you miss the centre. But I who have had to listen to your ramblings hit the middle first time. What have you got to say now beggar man?'

The beggar asked Lu Sei if he could hit anything he cared to name with the same accuracy he had hit the target.

'Anything you care to name I can hit. But then why should I want to prove myself to a beggar such as you?'

'If you could hit a bird in flight then I would clean your house and tend your garden free of charge for one year.'

This was an appealing offer, so Lu Sei said, 'Beggar man I accept your offer, but first you must know that when I was younger I could shoot birds out of the sky blindfolded.'

The beggar replied, 'I do not ask you to be blindfolded, all I ask is for you to shoot the bird under conditions that I shall arrange.'

'Name any condition you like,' replied Lu Sei. 'It will not alter my aim.'

'Just one more point,' said the beggar. 'What do I get if you fail?'

'In that unlikely event you can, within reason, name your own price,' replied Lu Sei.

'My price will be for you to seek out a Zen archery master and study with him for the same amount of time I would clean your house if I lose the bet.'

They both agreed to the terms of the wager. The beggar led Lu Sei off towards the woods and up a narrow mountain path until they came to a small clearing at the top of the mountain.

'Right,' said the beggar, 'the test begins here.' He led Lu Sei to the edge of a cliff and got him to stand with his heels on the edge and his toes sticking out over the empty space below. By now Lu Sei was perspiring greatly as he was already seized with vertigo and his hands were visibly shaking.

'Now raise your bow and shoot at any passing bird you see,' said the beggar. 'You can even choose your own target. It can be a big bird or a little bird, I don't care. Just choose one and then shoot it out of the sky.'

Lu Sei couldn't have cared less about birds, archery, beggar men or anything. He felt that at any moment he was going to topple over the edge and fall to his death on the rocks far below.

'You win! You win!' screamed the quaking Lu Sei, and with that he stepped quickly backwards away from the edge. The beggar looked at the shattered state of the once arrogantly assured Lu Sei.

'Kyudo is more than just skill with a bow. It is about cultivating the mind also. Your aim should link with your mind and concentrate on the point beyond the target. You should be oblivious to all around you. On the battlefield you cannot run when the enemy fires their arrows at you. Kyudo is an art beyond technique, it transcends fear and danger. Your mind should be focused and stay focused. Remember that great winds are powerless to disturb the water of a deep well, and the blind do not fear snakes.'

Lu Sei upon hearing this wisdom was duly shamed and realised that his way of the bow was the wrong way. The two then walked back into town and the beggar gave Lu Sei the name of a master that would aid him in his true quest.

The Fight
of
No Fight Style
II

One day a great master of the sword was taking a ferry ride down the river to meet a boyhood friend who was another master of the martial arts. They met every now and then to eat and drink and talk of old times. During the ferry ride, the sword-master sat quietly looking at the riverbank and con-templating upon how good life was, and how happy he was being a teacher and moulding young minds into the way of the sword.

On another part of the ferry there was a gang of young men shouting and drinking, and generally behaving extremely badly. The gang annoyed one party of travellers and then another, all the time working their way up the ferry towards the master. About halfway through the ferry ride the rowdy youths reached the old man and had begun to taunt

him. At first he appeared oblivious to the proceed-
ings, for he was just happy contemplating nature.

'Hey old man!' one of the youths shouted. 'Move
over we want to sit there.'

'So sorry,' the old man replied, then he stood up
and moved along to make way for the rowdy youths.
As it was about lunch time he opened up his bento
('lunch box') and began eating some pickled radish
and rice.

'Hey old man!' the same youth cried. 'Give me
your food I am hungry too.'

The old man looked up and, smiling, offered the
youth part of his lunch.

'I want it all,' said the youth. 'Can't you see I have
my friends with me.'

The old man replied, 'You are welcome to half of
what I have, but I am also hungry.'

The youth reached out and attempted to snatch
the bento from the old man. A subtle move by the
swordmaster and a shift of body weight left the youth
snatching at fresh air, then he toppled over on to the
deck.

'You will die for that, you stupid old fool!' The
youth began to pull his sword from its scabbard. By
this time, the captain of the ferry had been called and
appeared on the scene.

'What's going on ?' he enquired.

The youth turned around to face the captain and said sneeringly, 'Why Captain, I'm about to teach this old man a lesson he will never forget.'

'Do you know who that old man, as you call him, is?' asked the Captain.

'No, who is he then?'

'That my hasty, hot-tempered friend is the famous Tsukahara Bokuden, the finest swordsman in all Japan.'

The youth laughed out loud, as did his comrades. 'He doesn't look as though he could lift a sword let alone wield one.'

By now the youth had pulled his sword completely out of its scabbard and pointed it tauntingly at the old man.

'Come on old man, fight me and let's see what you can do. Tell me what your style is, so that I will know how inferior it is after I kill you.'

'My style is that of the No Fight Style,' the old man quietly replied.

'No fight!' jeered the youth. 'I have not heard of that school before. It must be a sword school for old men and cripples.' And with that derogatory comment the youth burst into laughter.

The situation now looked serious. The old man knew that no matter what he did the youth was spoiling for a fight and would not let up until he got one.

'If we fight on this ferry the confined space will inhibit our movements, and also we could injure some passengers.' The old man then pointed to an island a few hundreds yards up river. 'I think we should go to that island and fight there.'

The youth gracelessly agreed. The captain allowed them to borrow a rowing boat and they rowed towards the island. The youth was first out of the boat, almost drawing his sword at the same time, so eager was he to finish off the old man.

'Wait,' said the old man. 'Is it not customary to stand back to back, walk twenty paces and then turn before we start to fight?'

'Have it any way you want old fool. You're going to die whatever we do.'

The youth stormed off up the beach, counting loudly up to twenty. At twenty he turned around with his sword raised in the air, only to see the old man merrily rowing back to the ferry. The youth cursed and screamed, but all to no avail.

'With my No Fight Style one is the victor of a thousand battles!' shouted the swordmaster.

Tsukahara Bokuden knew that his skill with a sword was unsurpassable and so had saved the life of the youth, though the youth did not know it, by using a simple ruse.

The
Forty-Seven
Ronin

Π

One of the most famous legends of the martial arts is that of the forty-seven ronin. Ronin were samurai without a lord and master. They have wrongly been likened to mercenaries.

Some time around 1702, during the period in Japanese history known as the Tokugawa Shogunate, the shogun (military leader of the country) chose two lords to help him entertain some high-ranking officials from the Emperor's court in Kyoto. Because these two lords had lands in the country their knowledge of court procedure and etiquette was a little too basic. So the shogun asked one of his own officials, a Lord Kira, to teach them the necessary ceremonial duties, so that everything would run smoothly and the shogun would not lose face.

Japanese society in those days was run in strict

accordance with certain rules of good form. Even the slightest wrong move by a retainer or servant could result in a severe loss of face for their employer and family. Almost always, punishment was death because death to the Japanese was the only method of apology to an offended party.

According to custom, the two lords in question would give Lord Kira a small gift from each of them for taking up his valuable time. Lord Kira was a much disliked man even amongst his own kind and never had a smile or a good word for anyone. He felt that the presents given to him were inadequate and worthless. Although loss of face prevented him from telling the two lords this, he was overheard bemoaning the affair to his concubine by a retainer of one of the lords.

The retainer quickly relayed the information to his master. The Lord believed that, as a result, his house was in danger of falling from favour, so he secretly gave his servant a large sum of gold to give to Lord Kira. Unfortunately, the other country lord, whose name was Asano, had no knowledge of how the Lord Kira felt about him, or of what the other lord had done to restore favour. Kira, very happy with the bag of gold, felt that the other lord should also do the same. But he knew he could not ask him because again it would show loss of face. Instead he began to insult Asano, calling him poor and cheap, and scorning him for his lack of knowledge regarding courtly etiquette.

Kira's behaviour to Asano could have only one outcome according to the strict samurai code of the preservation of honour – Lord Kira's death. Asano found his opportunity during another lesson when Kira commented in front of others at the slowness of Asano's mind in understanding court protocol. Lord Asano sprang at Lord Kira with a dagger in his hand and plunged it into his sarcastic instructor's body. The blow it turned out, however, was not fatal and Kira lived.

However, Asano had unsheathed a weapon in the shogun's palace and the punishment for such an offence was seppuku (ritual suicide, also vulgarly known as hara-kiri). He complied with the law and tradition and duly killed himself by the required method of disembowelment.

As a lord, Asano had a number of samurai retainers, forty-seven in all, who upon the death of their master became ronin. They were incensed at what had happened and vowed revenge upon Lord Kira, whose greed and insults had put their master in his grave.

They knew the shogun and other officials would be expecting retribution from them because of what had happened. So they pretended that their master's death called for no retribution. Each went their separate ways and were never seen together.

Secretly, they had planned to live their lives as normal but meet altogether exactly one year to the day from when the affair had begun. So on 14th December 1703 the forty-seven ronin crept stealthily through the night and made their way into Lord Kira's household unobserved. The snow on the ground had dulled their footsteps so that the household was taken by surprise. After some fierce fighting everyone in the house was killed except Lord Kira. He was found later by the ronin leader's son hiding in a cupboard. The ronin leader, Kuranosuke, ordered him to commit seppuku but the cowardly Kira would not do so. Taking a pace backwards, Kuranosuke drew his sword and with one clean blow beheaded him.

The decapitated head of Kira was then taken to the tomb of Lord Asano in the grounds of Sengaku-ji Temple and placed upon his grave. Retribution had been made. The ronin were then called upon, as they had expected, to commit seppuku for their deed, which they did. They were all buried near the tomb of their lord. It was the ultimate act of total dedication to their master. A celebration of this great deed is held every 14th December in Tokyo.

The
First
Sumo

Π

Japanese Sumo wrestling is over 2000 years old and is thought to be one of the oldest wrestling systems in existence, and maybe even a forerunner to the original martial arts. In ancient times most societies settled disputes through hand-to-hand combats. The first recorded sumo bout was written over 800 years ago.

In a town near Yedo there lived a giant of a man named Kuyehaya. According to him, he could out-eat and out-drink anyone, and even if you were to search the world over you would find no one who could compare with him for strength. It was said that he could straighten iron hooks with his bare hands and snap the horns off cattle with little trouble. The braggart would state these claims from dawn to dusk, day in and day out. His wrestling ability was incomparable, so much so that after he had killed more than forty opponents no one wanted to challenge him any more.

The emperor became tired of the constant petitions to the court from the villagers and townsfolk in the area complaining about Kuyehaya's frightening and obnoxious behaviour. So finally, he issued an edict asking for someone to come forward and contest the giant bully's claims.

Some six weeks later a man named Sakune offered his services. The emperor told him that if he could defeat Kuyehaya he would give him land and a small pension. So off Sakune went to challenge the boastful Kuyehaya.

People came from far and wide to witness this great fight, though nobody expected the unknown Sakune to beat the giant, but at least it would be a spectacle worth watching. On the day of the fight the two men faced each other, stamping their feet hard on the ground. Kuyehaya began by kicking his opponent in the ribs and breaking them. Sakune retaliated with a devastating kick to the groin, so hard was the blow that it completely smashed the area surrounding the groin killing Kuyehaya. The whole fight had lasted about twenty seconds.

Today, in Japan, that first sumo contest is honoured every 7th July at the place where it occurred.

What's in a Name?

Π

In medieval China most people lived in small villages and hamlets. The provincial government was so far away that the peasants often looked to the local priest, who was either Buddhist or Taoist, for help in an emergency. There was a village in Fukien province where the inhabitants had been experiencing a problem with a man-eating tiger that had been killing their livestock. The farmers in the area called upon the priest for help in tracking down and killing the tiger.

The priest, who was also a kung fu teacher, as priests often were, enlisted the help of his senior student in this daunting task. The two of them set out the next day to track down the man-eater, calling first at a farm to collect a lamb to be used as bait.

For three days they followed the tiger's tracks from

where it had last struck until they came to an area where the priest believed the tiger lived. The plan was to tie the lamb to a tree in a clearing and then wait for the tiger to appear. The priest decided that they should stand back to back, so that whichever way the tiger came one of them was sure to see it. The priest had instructed his student to use a spear hand strike to the tiger's heart which would kill it outright.

They stood in silence, back to back, for over eight hours. By the time evening was beginning to fall the student was feeling very tired. The priest on the other hand was still fully alert, as his years of meditation practice had accustomed him to such long periods of stillness. The student also felt fear creeping into his heart, because being so weary he felt that he would not have the strength to fight the tiger and so he would probably be killed.

Just then a rustling sound was heard in the bushes. Both men prepared for the impending attack of the tiger. Adrenaline was surging through the student's veins when suddenly an old man walked into the clearing. He must have been at least eighty years old. The priest advised him to get home as quickly as he could because there was a man-eating tiger about, which they were waiting to kill. The old man nodded and said that he knew about the tiger as it had attacked some hours ago and he had killed it. The priest and student stared at the little old man in total disbelief.

'How could someone like you so advanced in years take on a man-eating tiger and kill it? Why, you don't even have a weapon!' said the priest.

'I had my hands,' retorted the old man. 'What else should I need?' Then realising that they didn't believe him, the old man turned and walked away.

'What's your name?' the priest shouted after him.

'That is of no consequence,' replied the old man just before he disappeared from view.

The priest and the student didn't really believe what they had heard, but they still wanted to go and look in the direction the old man had come from. But it was by then dark and so they decided to leave the search until the morning. At dawn the next day they set off. Some three hours later they came upon a clearing and there on the ground was the huge carcass of a tiger. They could find no wounds on the body from spears or swords. However, there was a huge indentation in its back and so it was clear that the animal's back had been broken. Signs of a struggle near by indicated to the priest that the tiger had obviously jumped the old man from behind, and that the old man had thrown it over his shoulder snapping its back in the process. But there was no clue as to how he was able to accomplish such a feat!

The two walked back home to the village in silence. The priest thought to himself that the old man must have been a warrior monk with a style so secret and so effective that even he did not know what it was.

§

Patience is the Key

Π

There was once a great karate sensei called Majuro who lived on the island of Okinawa, which is in the Ryukyu Archipelago off the coast of Japan. He taught his art very differently from other senseis, and believed that philosophy and the art of the empty hand (karate) should be used in conjunction, with each complementing the other. His methods of teaching were always twice as long as other masters', but then the students he produced were twice as good as any other.

Over the years many prospective karate students knocked upon his door asking to be taught by the great master. Almost always they were refused. Majuro, it seemed, liked to pick his students himself.

One day he was visiting a herbal shop in the city when he saw a gang of youths taunting another boy who seemed to be giving as good as he got. Stopping to watch for a moment to see what happened next, he saw the group of youths set upon the lone boy in an attempt to beat him up. After about three or four minutes of fighting the gang left, leaving the lone boy brushing the dust off himself. Majuro walked across to the youth and complimented him on his bravery at taking on four fighters.

'You may not have won the skirmish,' he said, 'but you did not get badly beaten. I am a karate sensei and if you are willing to learn and ask no questions about your training, no matter what, I will teach you techniques that will equip you to fight four opponents with ease.'

The boy, whose name was Sato, eagerly agreed to become a student of this great master.

Once they had reached the sensei's remote house in the foothills of a small mountain range, Majuro laid down the ground rules to his newly acquired pupil. Sato was ordered that he must never ask about karate, must never speak about it and must never train by himself with what he knew already without the master's explicit instructions. He must obey every command that his master gave him no matter what it was.

For just over a year Sato would get up before dawn every day and fetch the water from the river in two big, heavy buckets – a trip of about two miles – then he would cook the master's breakfast before he started the washing. After cooking lunch for the master Sato would then gather wood for the evening fire and look after the garden. As dusk came he would prepare the evening meal and get more water from the river. Most nights he would retire to his bed totally exhausted. He never asked why he had to do all these chores, or mentioned a word about karate training to his master.

One day, Sato was in the garden working away in the radish patch when Majuro came up quietly behind him and gave him a vicious blow with the branch of a tree. Sato fell to the ground, rubbing his head. The next day whilst cooking the breakfast Sato suddenly received another terrible blow to the back of his head, and turning round he saw his master walking away. The master put his finger to his lips and said, 'Remember, no questions!'

Day after day, month after month, in every part of the house and garden Sato was attacked by his master with the tree branch. By the time another year had passed the slightest sound, even that of a petal dropping from a flower, had Sato on the balls of his feet ready to dodge the impending blow. Nothing else in his life mattered; for Sato there was only a constant, total readiness. The master then approached his student and said to him, 'Now you are ready to learn karate.' And five years later the people in his home town were calling him 'Sato the unbeatable'.

§

The River Workers' Lunch

∏

The late Grandmaster Yip Man was the modern-day keeper of the flame of the Wing Chun kung fu system. The martial arts world owes a debt of gratitude to him and the late Bruce Lee. As a young man Grandmaster Yip had many encounters with street fighters and the following story is of one such encounter.

One day, Yip Man and his little son, Ip Chun, boarded a ferry to cross the river to travel to his home town of Fatshan. One of the passengers was a huge Chinese cook who was carrying a large cooking pot filled to the brim with piping hot noodles. This was to be the lunch of the river workers on the other side. When the ferry neared the shore young Ip Chun was burned on the side of his face by the cooking pot, as the burly cook rushed past him in his hurry to disembark. The boy's father quickly followed the cook off the ferry and remonstrated with him about the injury to his young son. To which the cook retorted that the young lad should have looked where he was going. Yip Man was further insulted when the cook put down the cooking pot on the dockside and told him to shut up or he would throw him into the river.

By this time the hungry river workers, about seven or eight of them, had gathered around to see what the commotion was all about. Yip Man stood his ground and gently pushed his son, who was now next to him, to one side. One of the workers, obviously impatient for his lunch, shouted to the cook to throw him in the river and be done with it so that they could all eat.

The big cook strode forwards with his fists ready. Within the blink of an eye Yip Man had pushed his son further out of danger and at the same time sidestepped from the path of the oncoming attack. The cook lashed out with his foot then followed it with a punch. Yip Man blocked it with the famous bong sau block and punch combination. He then hit the cook squarely in the jaw and sent him reeling back to finish up on the boards of the jetty. Seeing their friend knocked to the floor, the river workers rushed forwards with the intention of finishing what the cook had started.

In a series of flashing hands and elbows, punctuated with a few swiftly rising knees, Yip Man felled the angry workers, one by one, like ninepins. Some went over packing cases, some were sent sprawling into the river and others just fell where they stood. The whole fight lasted less than two minutes and when the dust settled battered bodies lay scattered all around. Calmly, Yip Man dusted himself down, called for his young son and strode away to carry on with his journey, leaving in his wake a small crowd, staring in disbelief.

§

The Deadliest Man on Earth

II

Yip Man in his later years left Fatshan and headed for Hong Kong, where he remained for the rest of his life. He opened a kung fu school and began teaching a few students. One student named William Cheung began training in the wing chun system before he was ten years old. At that time Yip Man only taught the modified version of the style to his students. This particular version had been designed by another, earlier grandmaster called Leung Jan.

Leung Jan had had a slight problem at his kwoon ('school'). His son Leung Bik, although a good fighter, stood only five feet tall and was small-framed. For all his expertise in wing chun, his father thought, if it ever came to a duel for the head of the school after his death, then the most senior student, Chan Wah Shun, who was hugely built as well as a powerful fighter, would probably win. So, Leung Jan sought to eliminate the effectiveness of the footwork and limit the devastating arm techniques that he had taught Chan. The big student would then not be a threat to his son for the grandmastership. However, although the traditional version of wing chun is so much superior, Leung Bik was still defeated after his father's death by Chan Wah Shun and fled to Hong Kong.

Yip Man became a senior student under Chan, and he knew of the traditional version of wing chun and its superior effectiveness over the modified form. So, after training for four years with Chan he went to Hong Kong to find Leung Bik and complete the traditional training in the system with him.

When Yip Man opened his own kwoon, however, he too only taught the modified version of wing chun and nobody knows why. His prowess as a sifu ('teacher') and fighter spread far and wide, and it was at this school that William Cheung became a student.

After a few years of training, when he was about fourteen, Cheung decided to train full-time with Yip Man. This meant him leaving his home and living with his master. Perhaps a high price to pay for one so young, but his burning desire was to carry on and preserve the wing chun system, one of the greatest achievements of Chinese culture. Because of this ambition, Yip Man had chosen Cheung to be the only heir to the traditional version of the system. On the condition that Cheung would not pass on any of the secret knowledge in Yip Man's lifetime.

Throughout the 1950s the young Cheung won the kung fu elimination contests in Hong Kong against opponents with years more experience. It was due to his success that he became entangled with the Chinese Triads, who controlled most of the martial arts in Hong Kong. They were upset with Cheung because they considered it a loss of face that their finest kung fu fighters had been defeated by a young kid.

In 1959, due to life-threatening pressure from the Triads, William Cheung fled to Australia. Although when he first arrived he had only a poor grasp of English, he studied hard and eventually gained a place at Sydney University, graduating with a degree in economics and art. Throughout his five years of study he had to pay his own way, including schooling expenses.

In 1974, two years after Yip Man's death, Cheung began to teach wing chun professionally in Melbourne, freed from his vow of never revealing the full extent of the 'old art' whilst his master lived. Cheung realised that the time had come for him to share his knowledge with the world. He had also decided that the traditional taboo placed on the teaching of wing chun to non-Chinese was outdated and unjustifiably xenophobic. His expertise in the art became known the world over. At one time he held the world speed punching record of 8.3 punches per second, and to some he was known as the 'deadliest man on earth'.

§

Empty Hands versus the Yakuza

Π

After World War II Japan was in a state of great devastation. The American General MacArthur was supreme head of the US occupation forces and was doing his utmost to rebuild the country as quickly as possible. But the great turmoil across the land was felt from the humblest peasant to the governing classes. Everything was in short supply and the country's infrastructure would take time to rebuild. Most of the economy relied on the money spent by the US soldiers or Western aid. To the man on the street it appeared that the whole economy was run by the Yakuza (Japanese gangsters). The black market thrived and so, of course, did crime. Prostitution, protection rackets, smuggling, it seemed as though murder and mayhem had become the Japanese way of life.

The men of the defeated Japanese army slowly returned to their homes from allied prison camps all over Southeast Asia, with the ignominy of defeat still very much in their hearts and minds. The scene of devastation that met them was perhaps more than most could take. One such soldier, named Doshin So, vowed upon returning home that he would not rest until his own town was free from the grip of the Yakuza.

Doshin So had been a great martial artist in a style called shorinji kempo (shorinji is the Japanese translation for the Chinese Shaolin). He was no ordinary man and during the war he had been a special envoy in Manchuria and one of the government's top espionage agents. Even when Japan was defeated he avoided capture by the Russians in Manchuria and managed to return home, aided by members of a Chinese quasi-secret society called the Black Dragon. The allied forces had complete control over the whole of Southeast Asia in 1945 and so his feat of remaining undetected was quite remarkable.

Doshin So's home was on Shikoku, which is one of the four main islands that make up Japan. His home town of Tadotsu was, like everywhere else in the country, dominated by the Yakuza. Upon his return many of the young men of the town, knowing of his reputation as a great martial artist, looked to him for leadership. Doshin So began to train a small band of the local youth in the martial art of shorinji kempo. He set up a shortened learning programme, teaching his eager young students only the most devastating punches and kicks. He further instructed them how to kill and maim with just one punch or finger jab to a vital spot or nerve point. This was essential knowledge because the Americans had banned weapons of all kinds, but firearms were impossible to get hold of anyway. Armed only with their empty hands and martial arts expertise, Doshin So and his students took on the mighty Yakuza.

At first there were just small groups who fought night after night with the gangsters. They would raid one place and then another. Even though weapons were banned and hard to come by, the Yakuza were always armed with swords and a vicious looking dagger called a tanto. They fought with intimidation and kidnapping, but the Yakuza could not break the spirit of Doshin So's students. Some of the youths were killed almost immediately, others were maimed, but still they fought on against the evil that was the Yakuza of Tadotsu.

The Yakuza soon found that the amount of money they were making was falling at a rapid rate, so reinforcements were sent for from other Yakuza groups outside of Tadotsu. But as fast as they came the now growing band of students defeated them. One particular group of fifty gangsters did not even make it to the town. They were ambushed by the fighting and kicking shorinji students and sent back to where they came from.

From just a small group of dedicated martial artists grew a mighty army of fighting townspeople. Eventually, the Yakuza fled to the safety of the bigger cities. The fearsome Yakuza, the dread and scourge of Japan, had been taken on and beaten by a small group of youths inspired by their leader Doshin So.

Doshin So went on to establish a Chinese Shaolin monastery and incorporated into his growing movement philosophy, religion and the moral obligation to believe in one's own ability to overcome any obstacle. The monastery still stands on the outskirts of Tadotsu today.

§

The
Black
Assassins
Π

In Japan over a thousand years ago there lived a group of people called the ninja, who practised a secret art called ninjutsu. Trained from birth in remote mountainous regions, a ninja was the ultimate martial arts expert. Deadly in all forms of hand-to-hand combat and a master of the bow, sword, dagger, spear and a multitude of other weapons, their art was one of death by assassination and the very word ninja would send a cold shiver down the spine of peasant and samurai alike.

The ninja were garbed from head to foot in black, and their skills of espionage and murder were such that these warriors of the night were considered almost magical. The ninja warrior was a complete fighting machine. He knew no fear and would rather die than fail a mission. There are many myths and legends in Japanese folklore and martial arts history of their exploits over the centuries.

One such legend tells of three ninja who were sent out on a mission to kill the daughter of a daimyo ('feudal lord'). The daimyo was planning to marry his daughter to a rival lord in order to join the two families together and thus make them the most powerful alliance in western Japan. The ever-changing politics of the shogun meant that this overlord constantly needed gain support from friends and to forge alliances with other lords to maintain his supreme position in the land. The volatility of favour at the emperor's court meant that at any given moment a more powerful new alliance could suddenly appear.

The shogun knew that the marriage of the daimyo's daughter would unite two powerful families. They would then be strong enough to challenge his supremacy. To prevent this the shogun sent a messenger to negotiate with the chief of a ninja clan. He offered to pay a large amount of gold to have the daughter killed in such a way that the blame could be put upon the prospective husband.

The ninja accepted the job and because of its extreme importance sent out three ninja rather than the customary one. They set off one at a time, arranging to meet a month later to collate all the information they would have gathered about the lay of the

land, strength of the castle and the number of samurai retainers that the daughter of the daimyo would
have as a bodyguard.

As masters of disguise and subterfuge the ninja
could simply blend in with the community. One
ninja disguised himself as a ferryman, another as a
wine-seller and the third as a wandering Shinto
priest. The ferryman could pick up idle gossip from
travellers as they crossed the river. In those days travel was largely restricted to the upper classes, so it was
more than likely that some passengers on the ferry
would be wedding guests. The ninja disguised as a
wine-seller found a wine merchant from another district, killed him and all his family, burned the house
down and made off with a cartload of wine and two
horses. Everyone drinks wine at a wedding. The third
was a wandering priest and as such could go almost
anywhere without being challenged.

The trio had chosen their disguises well and were
never detected. At the changing of the moon a
month had passed and they all met up at the desig-
nated place to discuss their findings and make plans
to accomplish their mission. The wine ninja told of
how the castle was preparing for the wedding feast.
The ferry ninja spoke of the number of samurai that
always accompanied the daughter. The priest ninja
told of his wanderings in the town, his invitation to

the wedding and also how he had formulated an escape plan for after the deed's completion.

It was arranged that one week before the wedding the daimyo's daughter and her friends would give thanks at a shrine at the edge of the woods and then ask the forest spirit to bless her forthcoming marriage. Her future husband would then arrive and, holding hands in front of the shrine, they would ask for a joint blessing. The ninja priest had agreed to offer the blessing at this sacred place. Afterwards there would be a picnic beside a nearby lake.

The priest ninja planned to take the couple after their premarital blessing to the water's edge. In the solitude and stillness of the early morning he would unite the wood spirit with the water spirit (a typical Japanese ritual of that era), then gently splash water over the happy couple, signifying that the forces of nature and of heaven were in agreement upon the forthcoming marriage. After this ceremony the friends would be called from both sides and the picnic would commence.

On the day, all went well. The priest ninja gave the blessing at the Shinto shrine and escorted the happy couple to the lake. The daimyo's chief samurai wanted to escort her, but was persuaded not to by the daughter after the priest had explained that someone else's presence during the water blessing may offend the gods. However, the chief samurai remained just out of sight in the bushes.

The priest led the couple down to the shore and they entered the water up to their waists. The ninja priest than began to splash water over the pair of them. The splashing was the signal for the other two ninja to spring into action. They had cut reeds earlier in the day from the rushes of bamboo and so could remain under water by breathing through these hollow tubes.

One ninja swam under the water to where the couple were standing and unseen he gripped the girl's feet and pulled sharply, dragging her off balance and under the surface. The girl, frightened out of her wits, struggled violently but to no avail. The second ninja swam out to meet his colleague and together they held her under the water until her body went limp.

On the shore, pandemonium was breaking out as the prospective husband cried out and the chief samurai came running from the bushes. The ninja priest told the young man that the water spirits had taken the girl because the solemn blessing had been spied upon by the chief samurai. Seeing the body-guard now running towards him, sword drawn, the youth grabbed his own sword from where it lay on the shore and ran to meet him. The youth fell mortally wounded and soon the samurai from both families turned upon one another. A bitter battle ensued. The larger force of the daimyo routed the other samurai and seemingly won the day. By now the body of the girl was floating on the surface of the lake, just a few feet away from the water's edge.

It was a sombre group that arrived back at the castle. The priest told the daimyo that during the blessing at the water the young man, who had been drinking, had tried to become amorous with the girl. She, fearing that the water gods would be offended, resisted his advances and lost her footing in the struggle. She fell into the lake and most likely got trapped in the weeds that lie close to the shore. The chief samurai went on to say that upon seeing her disappear under the water he ran to her aid, but the young man was running towards him brandishing his sword, so he defended himself and killed him.

Grief-stricken, the daimyo accepted this account of events as true and so broke all ties with the other family. He sent messengers to the shogun telling him that he was ready to form an alliance. As for the ninja, they just disappeared back into the shadows from whence they came.

When the Buddha Called

Π

The Chinese new year doesn't begin on 1st January, as it does in the West. They calculate their years from 2637 BC, the year in which the legendary Yellow Emperor, Huang-ti, worked out a cycle of sixty years which lies at the centre of calendrical study. New year in China therefore does not fall on the same day each year, but sometime between 21st January and 20th February. So most Chinese festivals follow the lunar year.

The Lion and Dragon Dances, which are an important part of the Chinese new year celebrations, are only ever performed by kung fu students. Given the weight of these sturdily built wooden effigies it is perhaps only sensible that fit young men should carry them.

The Chinese assign a certain animal each year.

One year it could be the year of the Ox, the next the year of the Dragon. This naming of years came about, so legend states, when the Lord Buddha was dying. As he lay on his deathbed he wanted to give a blessing to all the animals of the world, so he sent out a request that they should come to him before he died. But when the time for his departure drew close, only twelve animals turned up to bid the Buddha farewell. In recognition of their loyalty he named a year after each one of them. Another legend has it that the fabled Jade Emperor wanted to hold a banquet for all the creatures of the earth. Invitations were sent out but only twelve turned up. Either way, the animals that did turn up were the Rat, Ox, Tiger, Rabbit, Dragon, Snake, Horse, Ram, Monkey, Cock, Dog and Pig. The order always starts with the Rat and ends with the Pig

The Leaping Leopard

Π

There was once a master of the Black Tiger system (a style well known for its heart-ripping techniques), who had a son named Wong Tau. One day, on his return from a hunt in the vast forests that surrounded their village, Wong's father brought home a half-starved baby leopard which he had found in the forest next to the carcass of its mother. He gave it to his son and told him he could keep the animal until it got too big and dangerous.

Wong and the leopard became inseparable and each day, after he had done his work around the house and practised his kung fu exercises, he would head off into the forest with the leopard to play. The weeks turned into months and the two were often seen by the villagers running together, wrestling on the grass or just lying peacefully in the sun, with each taking care of the other.

One day, whilst out enjoying themselves in the forest, Wong and the leopard were suddenly confronted by a large tiger. The tiger had been standing quite still watching them playing. Sensing the beast was about to attack them, the leopard began jumping around. The tiger was at least three times the size of the pet leopard, but the leopard, showing no fear, placed itself between the tiger and the boy. Standing its ground, the leopard seemed to tighten up its body so that every muscle was rock hard, but remained motionless waiting. Wong watched as he slowly but carefully walked backwards. He felt as though his leopard was waiting for something. The leopard was; it was using its instinctive cunning by patiently waiting for the tiger to leap.

Suddenly, the tiger launched itself at the tightly balled up leopard. The leopard also leapt and with perfect timing hit the surprised tiger in the stomach with the force of a cannonball. The tiger went sprawling backwards and the leopard, continuing the arc of its leap, lashed out with its razor-sharp claws, raking the exposed chest and belly of the tiger. Wong stopped in his tracks and watched with wonder at the bravery and skill of his friend.

The tiger landed on the ground with a heavy thud, blood pouring from its wounds and fled into the forest. Wong embraced his friend the leopard. He could understand quite clearly now that strength can be overcome with cunning and complete control of one's body.

From that day on Wong studied every movement that his friend the leopard made: its speed, cunning, agility, springing capability, in fact every twitch of every muscle. Eventually, many years later he incorporated the moves of the leopard into his own kung fu system.

§

The Northern Mantis

Π

After the Shaolin Temple had been razed to the ground the Wah Lum Temple became the centre of kung fu training. It was a Taoist temple rather than Buddhist as the Shaolin had been. None the less, it also housed and trained fighting monks. It was to this temple that a sickly youth named Lee Kwan was taken by his parents in an attempt to build up the child to regain his health. In exchange for food, accommodation and kung fu training Lee Kwan was expected to clean and sweep the temple grounds, fetch water and grow vegetables in the temple garden.

After intense training and special chi gung breathing exercises, Lee Kwan began to grow stronger and fitter, and his health improved hundredfold. The abbot of the temple noticed that Lee, unlike many of the students new to the training, seemed to grasp everything that he was taught very quickly, even some of the more intricate techniques. So much so that the abbot decided to instruct him personally in his own style of Northern Preying Mantis. The years passed and Lee Kwan became an accomplished exponent of this very difficult and strong system of kung fu.

One day he was training in the temple garden when a fellow student, who had just returned from the nearby town, fell to the ground in front of him. Upon enquiring, Lee discovered that the student had been badly beaten up by the sifu ('teacher') of the local kung fu school. Enraged, Lee stormed off intent on revenge for this insult to the temple. The abbot cautioned him that this was not the way, commenting, 'Arrogance is too often the companion of excellence', and if he insisted upon revenge he could never again return to Wah Lum. However, the hot-tempered Lee Kwan was beyond reason and went to the sifu and picked a fight, which resulted in the death of the kung fu master.

Although this was a challenge match and the laws at that time were not severe for killing under such circumstances, a jail term would have to be served. So to escape punishment Lee fled to Shanghai. It just so happened that upon his arrival there was a big martial arts tournament being held. Lee watched with interest as the various masters vied with each other in bloody matches to become the ultimate victor.

As the days passed he noticed that a monkey stylist had been distinguishing himself against the other fighters. He took note that this fighter was clever and extremely sneaky, especially in the art of deceptive techniques. This time instead of impetuously striding forwards to challenge, as he would have done before, Lee analysed everything and considered methods of countering with his own mantis system. Within a few days he knew how to defeat this would-be champion.

Lee considered that the most difficult to combat of all the monkey techniques was the elusive monkey defence. Having found a way to do so, he was now ready to make his challenge. He'd studied his opponent rather than rashly running off to fight, having remembered some words of the abbot when he was in training all those years ago: 'A reflection on a pool of water does not reveal its depth.'

Lee Kwan challenged the monkey fighter and by using his improvised tactics to bewilder the man he won the day. Lee Kwan left Shanghai a good deal wiser. He now realised that true kung fu is not about revenge fights and being hot-tempered all the time. The true essence of a man is not in what he has but in what he does.

The
Great
Thief

Π

In the 1930s the Japanese invaded China and the islanders of Formosa (now Taiwan) prepared themselves for occupation. They were greatly frightened because they had heard many stories of atrocities on the mainland. Many of the rich planned to cooperate with the invaders so that they could keep their lifestyles. But a legendary Formosan kung fu master, Liao T'ien-ting, vowed to resist and harass the invaders at every opportunity.

Liao became the champion of the oppressed Formosan people. The puppet government the Japanese had put in place to rule the island and which also helped the Japanese in their war effort was well aware that Liao was responsible for the attacks on Japanese officers. So, in an effort to placate him they tried to recruit him over to their side with offers of money and power.

Fiercely patriotic, Liao refused everything they tried to tempt him with. On one occasion he emerged from the bushes along a track in the jungle to surprise a Japanese officer and six men out on patrol. The officer was stunned to see this little man just appear before them, and went to draw his pistol. Before his hand even reached the butt of his gun his arm was dangling by his side, having been broken by a sidekick from Liao. The soldiers raised their rifles but Liao head-butted the first, kneed the second in the groin and grabbed the third soldier by the throat and turned him around to face his companions. He then broke the neck of the soldier and throwing his body towards the other soldiers disappeared as quickly as he had come.

The Japanese were furious at what this little kung fu man was achieving on the island. They sent soldiers after him but they had no success in finding him. He was a hero to the people, and the money and goods he stole were handed out to the poor villagers. No one would ever inform on him. Liao's raids on the homes of the rich merchants and Japanese officers increased and seemed unstoppable. The Formosan businessmen who had been co-operating with the Japanese hired top martial arts fighters and bodyguards to protect them. But the attacks continued and the bodies of these so-called protectors were generally found either dead or unconscious.

Liao's prowess as a skilled and deadly kung fu fighter was such that once when he was cornered in a tavern by a dozen, armed Japanese soldiers he single-handedly fought them and escaped. Every Formosan knew about their Great Thief (as the Japanese called him) and what he was achieving against the invader.

The military and the puppet government labelled Liao a thief and offered a large reward for his capture, but no one betrayed him. Bounty hunters came from the mainland to try to eliminate him and claim the reward, but few returned home. Many stories were told of how Liao would scramble across rooftops in the darkness and enter the most heavily guarded homes. Once it was rumoured that he even sneaked into the Japanese military governor's home, past all the guards and stole many items. The shame of the Japanese was considerable.

Sadly, however, Liao T'ien-ting was in the end betrayed by a distant member of his own family, who was too tempted by the great reward the Japanese were offering, and the great hero was executed. But to this day his system of kung fu is still practised by a dedicated few.

Fist
of the
North Wind

II

In the old days of kung fu, when a student became proficient in a style he would leave his master and open up his own school. To attract money-paying students a new teacher had to gain a reputation as a great fighter. This is how the challenge matches first began. One school would challenge another and more often than not, unless a rematch was successful, the losing school would probably close down. The history of the martial arts is full of such events.

One famous challenge took place many years ago between Ku-Yu-Cheong, who was a master of the Iron Palm and Tam Sam, a great fighter in the style of Choy Li Fut.

Master Ku, the more renowned of the two, had never been challenged before simply because his powers of iron palm were such that everyone feared that one touch from his hands, however slight, would kill them instantly. This was in spite of the fact that to look at, this master of the deadly iron palm, didn't seem at all dangerous. He was short and very thin.

The master had demonstrated his powers on many occasions by performing all manner of feats. Once he slapped a wild horse just once and the horse dropped down dead. It was discovered later that its internal organs were terribly damaged. Ku would also place up to twenty roofing tiles in a pile and slap the top one with what appeared to be just a light tap. The tiles would be smashed into fragments barely the size of a yuan (Chinese coin).

Tam Sam was the leading student of Chang Hung Sing, who was the founder of the hung sing style of choy li fut. This was a combination or joining of choy and li styles of kung fu.

When the day of the fight came neither fighter could gain the advantage over the other. Master Ku would strike with his deadly iron palm, but Tam Sam, with his tricky footwork, was never in the same spot twice, and so the deadly blows would always miss him. Tam would then retaliate with his long fist and Master Ku would deflect it, but he was never long enough in contact with his opponent's hand to employ the iron palm. After four or five hours of continuous fighting the two protagonists declared a draw. Each congratulated the other on their respective talents and became good friends.

Such a result was not unusual amongst kung fu fighters of the day. But what was unusual is that both men began to train together to learn the other's style. They then sent students on an exchange with one another and so gradually a new style began to emerge. The elements of choy li fut combined with Master Ku's iron palm from the northern Shaolin disciplines were combined to form the bak-sing ('north wind') style of choy li fut.

§

Ninja
versus
Ninja

II

Hanzo Hattori was the great chief of the Iga ninja clan. The Iga along with the Koga clan were the most powerful in all Japan. Of all ninja leaders Hattori was the most clever and he soon realised that an emerging general of the time, Tokugawa Ieyasu, had plans to become shogun (supreme military ruler).

Ieyasu made it known that if the ninja were to help him he would reward them once he became shogun. The incumbent shogun died two years later and so Tokugawa Ieyasu claimed his position and quickly established his authority. However, Japan was in absolute turmoil at this time. Everywhere daimyos ('lords') were in revolt, and in the north rebellion and insurrection were rife.

Once more Ieyasu contacted Hanzo Hattori and his ninja. He knew that he needed a vast network of agents to keep him informed about what was going on around the country. The Iga ninja began a large-scale operation, infiltrating castles, forts and all military establishments outside of the new capital of Edo (now Tokyo), reporting back news and events to Ieyasu about dissident nobles.

Thus Hanzo Hattori found himself elevated to the higher echelons of power inside the government. Ieyasu with his ninja agents was able to stamp out all insurrection. During this period, the ninja warriors were kept very busy spying on and carrying out assassinations of feudal lords that would not comply with Ieyasu's rule. This period in Japanese history was the beginning of the era known as the Tokugawa Shogunate.

Hanzo Hattori was appointed personal bodyguard to the shogun and was also responsible for setting up a government secret service. This superb spy system meant that Ieyasu and Hattori were always aware of dissidents long before they could ever become a serious threat. Usurpers could be quickly removed by despatching a ninja to make the problem disappear. Within five years Japan had been sealed off from the rest of the world because Ieyasu had issued an edict closing down the ports. The country was now effectively a fortress in reverse. Rather than preventing anyone getting in, the idea was to stop people getting out.

Among Hanzo Hattori's many titles was Chief Military Adviser, and it was in this capacity that he went with a force of ninja to Japan's Inland Sea to take care of a problem that had arisen. It seems that there was a seafaring ninja clan, the Fuma Kainin, that was raiding villages and shipping up and down the coast of the Inland Sea. These so-called pirates were becoming a menace, and so the shogun had despatched Hanzo Hattori to deal with them.

Hanzo's small fleet was made up of the local fishermen, as their expertise in sailing was far superior to that of land-based ninja. Hattori found the pirates, gave chase and cornered them into a small bay. He blasted their ships with black powder mortars and cannon. The victory looked complete and the battle of the ninja versus ninja almost won, but the ninja pirate chief had other ideas. He had spied Hattori on the bridge of his flagship, so he set fire to one of his own ships and let it drift towards Hattori. Sensing the danger the fire ship presented, Hattori ordered his fleet to withdraw.

Unbeknown to Hattori small groups of Fuma Kainin ninja had swum underwater to his ships and dismantled many of the rudders. These ships could not be moved out of the way of the fire ship. All Hanzo's crews could do was to abandon the ships and swim for it. This is when they got their second surprise. They found that the whole of the bay was covered in oil. The Fuma Kainin ignited the oil and within seconds the whole bay was aflame, engulfing Hanzo Hattori and his ships.

Thus the great ninja chief who had helped to build an empire died at the hands of another ninja clan.

§

The Overflowing Cup

Π

The philosophy of Zen has a deep significance when applied to the martial arts. A beginner or novice enters the place of training with a head full of opinions and thoughts, but part of the discipline is to empty the mind so as to become a vehicle for new learning. In essence, to be truly open-minded.

There is a story about an old Japanese Zen master who was engaged in conversation with a prospective student. The student chatted on and on, full of his own opinions and ideas. He described to the master everything he knew about Zen, trying to impress the old man with his great knowledge. The master sat and listened patiently for a while, then suggested that they take some tea. The student held out his cup dutifully and the master began to pour. The tea came to the top of the cup, but still the master kept on pouring.

The tea overflowed but still the master kept pouring. The student, unable to contain himself, pointed out that no more tea would go into the cup. The master looked up and said: 'Like this cup you are full of your own desires and ambitions. How then can I show you Zen unless you first empty your cup?'

Zen is, of course, a Buddhist concept and was strictly adhered to by the samurai. The Chinese who follow a complementary religion to Buddhism, Taoism (pronounced Dow-ism) would perhaps have said to the same student: 'Man cannot discover new oceans until he has the courage to lose sight of the shore.'

Many different philosophical concepts were used as tools by karate and kung fu masters in order to elevate the student to a place in his mind that is beyond fighting, beyond violence, and so towards a path of enlightenment and greater understanding.

§

The Invincible Warrior

Π

Miyamoto Musashi, who has already appeared in previous stories, was perhaps the epitome of the Japanese samurai, though strictly speaking he should be termed a ronin because for most of his life he had no master. He wandered across Japan in search of opponents to fight, and worked and studied continuously for both martial and spiritual perfection. By 1614 his reputation was such that few swordsmen would meet him in a duel. Musashi now believed himself to be invincible and so stopped using live blades (real swords) and took to using a bokken (wooden sword). A bokken is made from Japanese hard oak, a heavy wood, and such a sword could easily crack open a man's skull.

One of Miyamoto Muasashi's greatest duels was when he fought with a bokken against Sasaki Kojiro.

This young man had developed a very strong sword technique known as the Swallow Counter. It was a fighting move inspired by observing the motion of a swallow's tail whilst in flight. Kojiro, then a young samurai, incorporated his observations into his fighting technique and became unbeatable. He was taken into the employ of the lord of Bunzen province, Hosokawa Tadaoki, as a personal retainer.

Muasashi came to hear about Kojiro, so he travelled to Bunzen to seek permission to fight him from Hosokawa Tadaoki, as only he who could sanction such duel. Permission was granted and a time of eight o'clock the next morning was given as the hour for the duel. The place of fighting would be a small island a few miles outside the town of Ogura. Legend states that the evening before the match Muasashi changed inns, which led to the rumour that he had run off afraid for his life and in awe of the young samurai's skill.

As Muasashi sat in the small boat and was rowed across to the island, he picked up a spare oar and began to fashion a bokken from it. Once that was done he lay down and calmly went to sleep. The boatman woke him as they neared the island. Musashi began to tie back his hair with a towel and folded back the sleeves of his kimono, for ease of movement, and held them in place with some string.

As the boat hit the beach, Muasashi raised the wooden sword above his head and slipping into the water ran the last few yards with the waves splashing around his ankles.

Still running when he reached the beach he charged the group of people that had gathered around Kojiro. Stepping quickly to the side, Kojiro drew his long sword and waited for Musashi to reach him. By now, though still running, Musashi had dropped the wooden sword to his side. Kojiro seeing the opening, and expecting Musashi to be less than composed because he had run to meet him, made the first move and struck out at his opponent. This first cut went upwards and sliced through the towel upon Musashi's head. Musashi brought his wooden sword up in a perfect arc and then down, splitting Kojiro's head open from the crown to the shoulder blade.

As Kojiro's body fell on to the beach, the blood from his head spilled out over the sand. Musashi bowed to the people who had come with Kojiro and then turned and ran back to the boat. From that day on, Miyamoto Musashi only ever used a bokken when fighting duels.

Daddy's Scissors

Π

When the Portuguese arrived in Brazil on 1st January 1502, landing where Rio de Janeiro ('River of January') is now, little did they know they would be instrumental in founding a devastating martial art.

To colonise their new land and create plantations, the Portuguese did what the rest of the western European powers were doing at the time when they wanted cheap labour – they bought slaves. Over the following 200 years tens of thousands of African tribesmen were transported to Brazil.

The slave owners were cruel and heartless and worked their slaves to death. For those that did manage to escape there was the dense rainforest to face, with its ferocious animals and dangerous tribes. Many died within hours of running. Those which were captured were tortured and horribly mutilated as examples to the other slaves. By 1656 nine-tenths of the population of colonised Brazil were black slaves. The white traders and slave owners were very much aware that the chance of a revolt or uprising was extremely likely, so they petitioned the king of Portugal for more soldiers and formed their own militia. Then for the next few decades nothing happened.

The slave owners began to get complacent and the authorities refused to recognise that the blacks had the will or ability to fight. What they did not know was that over a hundred years earlier the black slaves had formulated a method of fighting by pooling their knowledge from various African fighting systems. People from all over Africa had been enslaved, including Zulu, Eboe, Bantu and Swazi warriors. Generation after generation passed on the style between the slaves of different plantations. Each student was sworn to secrecy under an oath of blood.

They called their new fighting art capoiera. Unlike other fighting systems, the movements of capoiera were limited by the fact that most slaves were chained hand and foot twenty-four hours a day. So the pattern for the fighting technique had to be formulated around restricted body movement. It was this that made the art of capoiera so unique.

Through experimentation, the slaves learned to

combine three elements to make their technique work: muscular strength, joint flexibility and rapid movement. They learned to flip their bodies into handstands and strike outwards with their hardened feet. Once the moves had been perfected the slaves then practised, in what little spare time they had, by first smashing gourds with their feet and then coconuts. With practice, these double-foot blows had tremendous force and deadly accuracy. It was said that a capoiera man could strike with a double-foot blow into an opponent's body and smash their internal organs.

In the early 1700s the slaves revolted and, still in chains, overran plantation after plantation. Soon there was a vast army of martial arts slaves hacking down every plantation owner they could find and taking over small townships as well. The government responded by sending out huge armies to defeat the slaves, which eventually they did. But not before a large number of white settlers had been killed. In the end, the firepower of the soldiers was the deciding factor in the final defeat of the slaves.

The art of capoiera was outlawed immediately by law that stayed on the statute books of Brazil until 1965. The ringleaders of the slave revolt were put to death in agonising ways and then decapitated. Their heads were placed in strategic places all around plantation perimeters as a warning. Reprisals for the revolt made the slaves fear for their lives, but a staunch nucleus of capoiera men would not let the art die.

Capoiera training continued but now it was incorporated into African dances so that the slave owners would not become suspicious. Rather than use their own names, the teachers of the art gave themselves colourful titles taken from the techniques they taught, such as Banana Plant, Dragon Fish and, the most advanced technique of all, Daddy's Scissors. A specialist in this technique could hold razors or short knives between his toes, and with one body flip could slash the throat or rip open the stomach of an enemy. Remnants of this deadly dance of death still existed in some Brazilian jungle villages right up to the outbreak of World War II. A formalised style is still practised today, thanks to the efforts of the anthropologist Benjamin Muniz.

§

David and Goliath Japanese Style

Π

A short but stockily built Okinawan taxi driver walked back to his home with sad news. He had to tell his wife that his horse-drawn taxi business had collapsed, and by the time he had paid back his debt to the bank he would have no money left. Entering his house, he told his wife what had happened and she was equally sad. They had left the island of Okinawa in 1920 and come to Japan to find a better way of life. The husband, Chokki Motobu, had had a reputation for being a great karate fighter on Okinawa, having been trained by the legendary masters of the art. But in the 1920s most Japanese had barely heard of such a fighting discipline. This was the land of the samurai and the sword, of ju-jitsu and judo. What on earth was karate?

Motobu decided that he and his family would

move to Osaka and he would try to get a job there. Eventually, he managed to gain employment as a night watchman at a spinning factory, which would at least pay the rent of the small lodging house they were in. Over the months Motobu began to gain notoriety as a fighter, as he was forever getting into arguments over one thing or another.

One day his landlord came to see him and showed him a newspaper advert that offered a large sum of money to anyone who could defeat a mighty Russian boxer. Motobu knew he needed the money, and the landlord, knowing what a good fighter his tenant was, thought he would make some money on a side bet.

On the day of the fight a huge crowd gathered inside the tent where the bout was to take place. Motobu was in the ring leaning on the ropes when suddenly a trumpet sounded and an enormous gaijin ('white foreigner') entered the tent and headed towards the ring. Gasps were heard from the audience as this gigantic Russian climbed into the ring. Motobu did not show any sign of concern, he just remained leaning on the ropes.

It had been agreed that it would be a bare-knuckle contest and the winner would be the one left standing. The first round began with the Russian lashing out with jabs which Motobu managed to evade. The big Russian kept up the pressure, continually throwing uppercuts and lethal jabs, which, if they had connected, would have taken the little Okinawan's head off. By the end of the round Motobu had not attacked his opponent once. The Russian had been unable to land any of his punches and was now mad enough to rip his opponent in half in the next round.

At the start of the second round the Russian strode forwards to settle his dodging opponent once and for all. Within a split second Motobu, who earlier had not fought because he was assessing his opponent, now jumped into the air and struck the Russian on the side of his head, near the carotid artery, with a knuckle strike. The Russian fell to the canvas unconscious. The audience looked dumbfounded and wondered how this little man was able to defeat such a big man. The landlord collected Motobu's money off the fight promoter and handed it to him. The crowd were now all clamouring around the little Okinawan, asking him what was it he did and could they learn it.

Within six months the fight had given Chokki Motobu a reputation second to none. There was so much interest in this little-known art of karate ('way of the empty hand') that Motobu opened up a school and became a full-time karate instructor.

Committed to Death

Π

One day a farmer was taking the fruits of his labour to the village market, as he did every month. The noise and the hectic hustle and bustle gave the village a carnival-like atmosphere. He sold his merchandise and met up with his friends to keep their monthly appointment at the local tavern. The day wore on and the conversation between the farmer and his friends got louder and louder. Sitting just across from the merry group was the lone figure of a samurai who had just lost his post as a retainer due to his lord's death. He was now effectively a ronin, a masterless samurai. Looking at this ronin, it was easy to tell he was proud, strong and followed the Zen code of bushido ('way of the warrior').

The farmer, more than a little intoxicated through drinking too much rice wine, got to his feet and, staggering slightly, bade farewell to his friends. As he turned around the scabbard of his small sword swept across the ronin's table and knocked his plate of food on to the floor. Apologising profusely, the farmer offered to pay for another meal. However, the ronin stood up and challenged the farmer to a sword fight the following week, telling him that if he did not appear he would not rest until he found him. He then walked out of the tavern.

The farmer barely knew anything about fighting. He had had his sword with him purely to protect himself against animals or the odd bandit. Knowing that there was no way out of this challenge, the farmer went to see a local swordmaster and told him of his plight.

The swordmaster told him, 'One week is too short a time to learn how to fight, no matter what I can teach you. You must get used to the idea that in one week's time you are going to die.' The swordmaster then went on to say that if he followed his instructions to the letter, although he would die, he could perhaps kill the ronin in the process.

'I will only have time to teach you one cut', said the swordmaster, 'and one stance. When the ronin attacks he will test you to see what skill you have, so don't move. Don't go to meet him or cross swords, just wait. Only when he goes to make his killing cut will you make your move.'

The farmer resigned himself to the fact that in seven days he would be dead. However, he decided not go down without a fight, so he spent the week practising the one stance, one cut technique that the swordmaster had shown him.

When the time for the duel came both men faced each other and drew their swords. The ronin took his stance with his sword raised to waist height and pulled over to the side in a two-handed hold. The farmer simply raised his sword above his head and waited for the imminent encounter. The ronin moved in, slowly sliding one foot forward in front of the other rather than taking a step. He circled the farmer first one way and then another, once or twice pushing forward slightly in a threatening way which was merely a feint to goad the farmer. Still the farmer stood his ground and faced the ronin. He knew death was just a second away, but his mind was totally focused on his task of delivering the one cut.

For more than an hour the ronin switched back and forth around the farmer, looking for an opening to cut him down. The farmer remained statue-like with his sword seemingly frozen in the air above his head, eyes staring and strangely calm. He had accepted death and so there was no look of fear upon his face.

Suddenly the ronin stopped, lowered his sword and stepped back.

'Farmer,' he said, 'when I challenged you I saw you as nothing more than a peasant and did not respect you. But today I see that you have no opening in your defence for me to strike at without receiving a fatal blow myself at the same time, and you seem not to fear death. You have the spirit of a samurai and I salute you. For me the affair is over.'

The ronin bowed low, turned and walked away. The farmer, however, still stood motionless. His friends came over, wisely calling to him before approaching, and congratulated him for his bravery. The farmer seemed almost unaware of the events that had transpired, such was his total focus upon delivering his one blow. Nothing else mattered, not even death.

§

The Herbalist

Π

In the province of Kwantung there was a kung fu teacher whose knowledge of the internal systems of fighting (tai chi chuan, hsing-i, pa-kua) was considered to be the foremost in China. Many years before he had been part of the emperor's bodyguard in the Forbidden City, which only accepted the best of the best. He had fought many fights in many battles and had never been defeated.

One such confrontation took place in the mountains, when he single-handedly fought off a band of brigands that were raiding a local village. In the process the teacher was injured and two days into his journey home he collapsed and sank into a deep fever.

For nearly three days he wrestled with death alone on the mountainside, slipping in and out of conciousness. By the fourth day the fever had broken, he came round and recovery was certain. During the fevered lapses of consciousness, he had had many dreams. In these dreams he was wandering the land, observing nature in all its many glories. The teacher felt that a certain harmony and balance were missing from his life, so he went back to the emperor and begged his leave to retire from his service. The emperor reluctantly agreed, for the teacher had been his prized captain of the bodyguard.

After a few years of wandering throughout the vastness that is China, calling off and studying at the many monasteries along the way, the teacher decided to make his home in a small village he had passed through some months earlier near the Yellow River. Here he opened a small school and taught medicine, religion and martial training – the trinity that make up the martial arts. To correct the balance of his earlier life of fighting battles, he taught his students philosophy. The motto of his school was 'What can kill can also cure'.

As he was nearing the end of his days he began to wonder which of his students would take over the running of his school after his death. He decided that of the trinity, medicine was the most valued and he therefore took a small group of his senior students out into the forest and told them that this was the final test of their knowledge of medicine. He thought that the student with the most knowledge would be the right person to carry on with his teachings.

'I want you to go out and bring me back as many plants as you can that have no medicinal value whatsoever.'

The students went off into the forest and began their search. After two or three days most of the students returned, each with a few plants. On the fifth day, the last student appeared empty-handed and with a sad look upon his face.

The teacher looked at this student and smiled, 'He is the only one of you that is qualified to take over my teachings.'

§

That Which is Useless is Everything

Π

'Stupid, stupid, stupid,' rang out the voice of the senior student across the kwoon ('training hall'). He was teaching a class and pulled the offending pupil out of the line.

'You have been practising these techniques for years,' he said. 'So why do you keep getting them wrong? You are just useless, no good to anyone, least of all yourself,' shouted the senior student.

Then the master came into the hall to see what all the commotion was about and witnessed his senior student scolding the pupil in front of the whole class. When the class was over and the pupils had gone home, the master walked over to his senior student and asked him what the problem had been. The student told him that no matter how many times the pupil was shown the technique of blocking and punching with one hand he couldn't get it right.

'He really is useless Sifu ['teacher'].'

'Nothing under heaven is useless,' the master replied. 'Everything has its purpose and its place,' he went on to say. 'Could it be that you see the flaws in others rather than in yourself?'

'No Master,' replied the student. 'But what can I do with such a useless pupil?'

The master sat down and directed his senior student to sit as well. 'I will tell you a story that may help you find an answer to your question.'

'Many years ago a carpenter and his apprentice were travelling through the district finding work as they went along. One day they reached a village called Crooked Oak and there in the centre of this village stood a vast gnarled oak tree. It was so broad it could shelter three thousand oxen. It was at least a hundred spans of a man's hand in circumference and its lowest branches were fifty feet from the ground. The old carpenter didn't even as much as glance at the tree as he walked past. But the apprentice just stopped dead in his tracks and gaped open-mouthed at such a spectacularly enormous tree.

'Seconds later he ran to catch up with his master. He said, "Never in all my life have I seen such a wondrous tree, surely it must be the biggest and most splendid tree in all China."

"The tree is useless", replied the carpenter.

"Why is that?" exclaimed the apprentice.

"Its bark is so gnarled that you wouldn't be able to get a straight plank from it more than about five or six feet long. Its trunk is twisted so badly that nothing I can think of could be made from the wood that would be useful. No, apprentice, that is a totally useless tree." He went on to say, "When I was very young my father, who was also a carpenter, brought me through this same village and I too made the same comment as you. My father gave me the same answer I have just given you. It is a tree that is good for nothing except to stand there being useless." And with that the carpenter strode off with his apprentice following behind.'

The master just sat there for a moment, looking at his senior student.

Then the student asked, 'What has the old gnarled tree got to do with the pupil I berated?'

The master replied, 'That tree was wondrous to all that saw it, it grew great and mighty and could shelter ten herds of oxen because it was useless. It was no good for building with or for making anything. It had survived for nearly a thousand years simply because it was useless. Do you think it would have grown to that impressive size and lasted so long if it had been of any use to anyone?'

The senior student understood that something may appear to be useless to one person but it may be of value to someone else. He made an oath that from then on he would take extra care when teaching the pupil he had earlier called useless.

§

The Runaway Bull

∏

The island of Okinawa is a veritable treasure house of legends concerning the early days of karate. This birthplace of the 'way of the empty hand' was the home for most of the great karate masters whose styles are still with us today. One of the greatest was a man named Itosu Yasutune. His introduction to karate came at a very early age via his father. Born the son of a samurai in 1830, Itosu was alleged to have been born with a 'fighting spirit' that never left him until the day he died, eighty-five years later.

When he was sixteen years old his father took him to the great karate master of the times, Matsumura Sensei, who took one look at him and instantly accepted him as a live-in student simply because he saw the fighting spirit in the boy's eyes. For nearly ten years Itosu trained under his teacher day in and day out, never once complaining about the harsh regimen he had to endure in the name of his art.

Matsumura Sensei was a strict disciplinarian, demanding and getting unconditional obedience. The years went by and young Itosu grew into a strong, healthy man with a physique many envied. He was as tall and handsome as he was deadly efficient in the art of karate.

One day, around Itosu's 24th birthday, he thought he would travel to the city of Naha to watch the great bull fights. As he approached the city there was a great commotion and people were running everywhere. He stopped one panic-stricken person and asked what was happening. He was told that one of the great killer bulls had broken loose and was attacking everyone that got in its way.

'Which way did it go?' Itosu enquired.

'Well you don't think we were chasing it do you?' came the sarcastic answer.

Screams of 'Run for your life' were heard and Itosu could see the bull running down the road towards him. 'It's a mad bull!' came a cry from near by. 'Move quickly or it will kill you!' shouted another voice. The young Itosu continued to walk calmly down the road into the path of the oncoming bull.

The bull, seeing another victim, charged straight at him. But the wily karate man waited until a split second before deftly stepping to the side. As the mad beast passed him, he lunged forwards and grabbed it by its horns. The bull charged down the road with Itosu still hanging on. The crowd watched, stunned, as Itosu was slowly forcing the bull's head backwards by its horns. About a hundred yards further on the mighty beast dropped to the ground in pain and utterly exhausted because of Itosu's grip. Now on the dusty ground Itosu wrestled with the bull until the stockyard keepers came to take it back to its pen.

Everyone came across to congratulate Itosu for what he had done. But to him, it was nothing. The man with the fighting spirit became one of the most famous karateka ('one who does karate') on Okinawa. He was to have many battles in his lifetime and defeat everyone that came to challenge him.

§

Attack
on the
Bridge
Π

When the great Tokugawa Shogunate era finally collapsed in 1868, it marked the end of a military government that had been established 250 years before by Shogun Ieyasu Tokugawa. Japan was now on the verge of entering the modern world.

Great upheavals were taking place across the land as modernisation swept all before it. Edicts went out forbidding the samurai to wear their swords unless they were employed by the new government. The two-and-half centuries of enforced peace had seen a gradual erosion of many martial ways. It was even said that the new samurai were not of the same mettle as their forebears.

The Western powers were flooding into the country eager to aid Japan in her plans to modernise what was a largely feudal country. Everyone wanted a piece of the lucrative trade that such expansion schemes offered. Each power was anxious to be on the spot when trade deals were made with the new government, and so they established consulates and legations.

The old samurai ways were regarded by many as almost a religion. The surge of foreign powers into their homeland was thought of as an invasion that they were not allowed to repel. Large groups plotted in secret to foment distrust of foreign interference, and attempts were made to persuade the merchant classes and to some extent the lesser daimyos (lords) to join them. Unrest, they hoped, would lead to rebellion and perhaps a return to the old ways. Already the cry was heard, 'Drive out the Barbarians!'

Three years earlier the British Legation had been attacked and a few days later one of its residents was caught by some fanatical samurai when out riding and pulled from his horse and hacked to death. Reports of other attacks and the deaths of several foreign diplomats were becoming all too common. The Western powers demanded action and protection from the new government.

Great Britain's envoy to Japan was Sir Harry Parkes, and he had made no secret of the fact that he was a hundred per cent behind the new Emperor and Japan's efforts to modernise.

Radicals within the samurai groups were aware that because of Great Britain's huge Empire, people like Sir Harry Parkes could influence those in Japan who were undecided about which path they should take. A plan was hatched to attack and kill this outspoken foreign barbarian before he could have his first audience with Emperor Meiji. Parkes was assigned two Japanese bodyguards who were samurai and ordered never to leave him alone. One of the samurai was named Goto Shojiro and was renowned as a great exponent of the sword, bow and hand-to-hand techniques. When Parkes was summoned to the Emperor's palace for his first meeting, he was accompanied by Goto Shojiro.

As Parkes and Goto rode through the streets of Kyoto at around dusk, they approached the bridge that led to the palace grounds. Suddenly, out of the shadows appeared three hooded assassins. Goto immediately sensing the danger, almost before the three hooded men appeared, leapt from his horse, sword already in his hand and with one mighty downward strike decapitated one of the assailants nearest to Parkes. Immediately spinning around, his sword gathering momentum, he slashed across the other two hooded figures as they continued to approach Parkes. One assassin fell dead, the other, mortally wounded, staggered off.

Parkes, who had only just realised what had happened, was visibly shaken. Goto remounted his horse and resumed the journey as though the incident had been a minor inconvenience. When the incident was reported, Sir Harry Parkes went on record as saying, 'The sword took his head off in a single stroke. A feat I would not have thought possible without considerable practice.' For the rest of Sir Harry's term in Japan, the samurai Goto was always seen by his side.

§

Petals
of
Death
Π

There was once a great daimyo (lord) of the northern provinces named Asano. He was very powerful because of the lands he owned and also because he could put into the field an army of fifty thousand men in less than a day. Although friendly to the shogun his potential as a future threat made the military government nervous. They felt that Lord Asano could control the balance of power. A decision was made that he had to be neutralised, but the problem was no other daimyo had a bodyguard as strong. Asano was protected around the clock and no one could even get near him and his home was a massive fortified castle. The shogun had no alternative but to send for the ninja.

A message was sent and soon a ninja jonin (high-ranking ninja) arrived to have secret talks with the shogun. It was explained that Lord Asano's death was imperative and the sooner the better. The military advisers told the jonin that a ring of steel surrounded Asano and his castle was impregnable, so it would be best to send a large force. Previous assassination attempts by mercenary ronins had all failed. The ninja negotiator just nodded and enquired about the sum of money concerned. Even by ninja standards the fee was enormous, but then so was the task. The jonin bade farewell to the shogun and headed deep into the forest to meet up with the next person in the chain of command, the chunin ('middle person').

It was the chunin's job within the ninja hierarchy to set the mission for the field ninja to carry out. Once the information had been passed to the chunin, the jonin went on his way. At the ninja stronghold, and after much consideration, it was decided that just one ninja would be sent out. It was felt that because of the paranoia of Lord Asano, a group would be more easily detected, whereas just one man could remain almost invisible. The lone ninja set off on his mission, carrying all the necessary equipment with him. What could not be easily carried was left behind, as the ninja field agent only had himself to rely on.

On arriving in Lord Asano's domain he quickly scouted around for a base in the woods to work from. Over the following weeks he watched and recorded every detail of Lord Asano's movements. He noted that upon rising the Lord would take a short walk around his garden, surrounded by his samurai bodyguard. To hide in a tree and shoot him with an arrow would be pointless as the arrow would hit his bodyguard. Asano rarely ever left the confines of the castle, and when he did it was always with a detachment of at least two hundred samurai. The ninja knew that if he was to succeed, then guile and subtlety would have to be his weapons.

One night, during a rainstorm, he crept into what he thought was the inner sanctum of the castle. But barely had he got two or three steps along one of the hallways when the floorboards began to creak loud enough to wake the dead. The surprised ninja realised that Asano, due to his constant fear of assassination, had installed 'nightingale' floorboards. These were boards constructed in such a way that any pressure upon them caused a high-pitched squeaking sound, so alerting the guards to intruders. Barely escaping detection the ninja fled and disappeared into the night.

The ninja had nothing left to try except his secret weapon, the power of the mind. From birth ninja were instructed in meditation techniques that almost bordered upon the supernatural. The ninja agent therefore sat in his hole in the woods near by the castle and sank into a deep meditation that lasted nearly thirty-six hours. By the time he came out of it, the ninja had devised a plan.

His next job was to search the woods and forests for a particular plant, which when the roots were boiled and filtered produced a deadly poison with no known antidote. In two days he had prepared the poison, worked out his route into the castle and the eventual time and place of death.

He waited until it was dark on the following day and then began his mission. He scaled the mighty walls of the castle again and avoiding the occupied parts of the castle headed for Asano's garden. In less than an hour the ninja was back in his hole in the woods with the trap set.

Next morning Lord Asano rose early as always and after washing went for his customary stroll in his prized garden. His samurai accompanied him with barely a hand's breadth between them and their lord. Asano spied that some new blossom had bloomed overnight and stooped down to inhale the fragrance, but after smelling the blooms he suddenly slumped to the ground, dead. His retainers thought their lord had suffered a heart attack, but the ninja had sprinkled a dusting of his deadly poison upon each blossom. He knew that the blossom would bloom the next day and that Asano would not be able to resist inhaling its scent.

Upon the ninja hearing the news that Asano was dead, waited for nightfall and then headed back towards the mist-covered mountains he called home.

§

The Invisible Hand

Π

In China's Shansi province they have a kung fu proverb, 'Correct hitting is invisible. The enemy should fall without seeing your hands.' It would seem that the kung fu masters of old expected great speed within the techniques they practised.

There is a legend about a feeble old peddler who some say 'walked like a man on his way to the grave'. It was said that he was of a great age and that he remembered when the dragons roamed the earth. His name was Pai Cheng and all he ever seemed to do was wander from village to village and town to town, selling his wares and also mending the odd cooking pot. Over the years many tales sprang up about Pai Cheng and the seemingly impossible feats he performed.

Once he was travelling along the great silk road

and was offered passage in a caravan for his own safety. He took the offer with a simple thank you and spent most of the journey asleep in the back of a yak wagon. About a week into the journey, when they were on a narrow mountain track, the caravan was suddenly set upon by one of the many groups of bandits who roamed the desolate hills and barren lands through which the silk road passed.

The bandits, about thirty in number, systematically cleaned out each wagon, taking the women as slaves, stripping the merchants of everything they had and killing the dozen or so guards that had been employed for protection. They finally came to the last wagon and found Pai Cheng soundly asleep. The old man had slept through all the fight quite undisturbed. A big man roughly awoke Pai and attempted to drag him off the cart. The bandit looked of Mongol origin and stood nearly seven feet tall.

'Come here you rag bag,' he shouted as he tried yet again to get a grip on the old man.

But with a subtle body movement, barely detectable, the old man avoided his grasp. By now the bandit chief and some of the others had made their way down the caravan and were laughing at the Mongol's attempts to get hold of the old man.

'If you don't get off, you will die where you lie.'

He then snatched a trident spear from one of the

other bandits and lunged forward. Again with almost just a twitch Pai moved out of the way. The Mongol tried several times but each thrust just missed the old man's head.

'Its like trying to spear a fish inside a cask!'

In the end the bandit chief dismounted and walked to the wagon.

'Get off now old man and your life will be spared, you have made great merriment and been a worthy adversary for my lieutenant.'

'Go away!' came the reply.

Time was pressing and the bandit chief wanted to be away. No longer laughing he ordered five of his men to pull the old man off the wagon and toss him over the cliff. Five bandits jumped into the back of the wagon and within seconds each came flying out hitting the ground with a thud. The bandit chief started to laugh again, taunting his men and calling them children. The laughter suddenly died on his lips when he found that the five bodies that had been thrown out of the wagon did not move. Closer examination revealed that all five were dead. 'How could this be?' he thought. He then stormed the wagon with a dozen of his men following up closely behind.

The rest of the people who had been in the cara-van could not understand what was going on at the rear of the train. The guards who had been watching them had hurriedly left to see what the commotion was. The caravan passengers and the merchants, divested of their clothes, slowly walked towards the rear. They were just in time to see three bodies go hurtling through the air and clean over the edge of the cliff.

Meanwhile, sword drawn, the bandit chief jumped into the back of the wagon and then, nothing, just total silence. The Mongol lieutenant looked worried, and then he too decided to mount the wagon. With-in a second a huge knife was at his throat and half the lower part of his shoulders were paralysed. Pai's grin-ning face looked out over the tailboard of the wagon. The Mongol, threatened with certain death, was unable to move and had a look of fear upon his face that told the remaining bandits he was about to meet his ancestors.

The old man shouted to the bandits, 'Your leader is dead because he would not let an old man sleep.' He then kicked the bandit chief's head out of the back of the wagon.

A gasp was heard from the bandits as they saw their leader's decapitated head fall to the ground.

Pai went on to say, 'Now you have a new leader, is he to die too?' Referring to the big Mongol with the knife wedged dangerously across his throat. 'I will give you one more chance to let an old man sleep. If you leave now and relinquish all you have taken, then nothing more will happen.'

The Mongol, barely able to move his head, garbled out something almost indecipherable, but it was enough to set the bandits throwing everything they had stolen on to the ground and release the women.

'Now go, and leave me alone!' shouted Pai.

With that he pushed the Mongol off the wagon and climbed back beneath the blankets. The Mongol, realising what a lucky escape he had had, quickly jumped back onto his horse and rode off. He was thankful he still had some men left and, of course, that he was now the new leader. So, at least someone had benefited from the raid.

Back at the caravan the merchants could not believe their luck. But then a thought slowly dawned upon them. How had one old man accomplished what the caravan guards could not? They went to the last wagon to ask Pai Cheng how he had done it, but he was sound asleep and they thought it prudent to leave him that way.

At their destination, Pai Cheng was the talk of the town. A plan to reward him was thwarted when they found he had left the city, telling the yak handler that the caravan was too noisy and too disturbing for an old man. He would make his own way.

Over the years that followed strange stories would be told about an old man carrying pots and pans who defeated outlaws and bandits all over China. The emperor got to hear of Pai Cheng and sent out emissaries to find him, but no one ever did. And yet, strange to relate, over fifty years later stories still abounded about an old pot seller who had saved people from certain death.

§

The Gentle Way

Π

When Jigaro Kano founded judo ('gentle way') he eliminated the self-defence techniques against an armed attacker. He further removed and barred the techniques based upon attacking the vital points of the body (atemi-waza), and also moves that involved bending and twisting the joints, with the exception of arm locks. He in fact created a sporting concept that is quite far removed from its core base of jiu-jitsu. Jiu-jitsu is a severe method of hand-to-hand combat on the battlefield. It was used by the samurai if ever they were cornered and lost their weapons, as a means of self-defence. An enemy could attack with dagger, sword, spear, in fact anything that could be used as a weapon.

Much has been written about a samurai's skill with a sword, but what is not generally known is that a samurai was equally expert in the martial arts of empty hands. Both aikido and judo owe their existence to jiu-jitsu. Legend relates that it was a certain Hisamori Takenouchi who founded jiu-jitsu in the early 1500s. He was a great samurai whose every waking moment was filled with training for the battlefield. The only empty hand combat methods that were around in his time were based upon sumo techniques.

Takenouchi had been part of a force that had been fighting against a rival daimyo ('lord') over a feud about land and borders. He had accounted for himself well in the ensuing battle, striking down many of the enemy with lightning blows of his sword. But he was hit in the shoulder by a stray arrow. As night fell Takenouchi regained consciousness and could hear the whispered voices of the battlefield jackals. These were the people that waited until a battle was over and both forces had departed and then would come out under cover of darkness to rob the fallen of anything that may be of value. Weapons, armour, money, even the actual clothes the warriors had worn would be stripped from their dead bodies. Quite often these jackals would come across a foot soldier or samurai that was only wounded and it was easier to plunge a dagger into them and so avoid a struggle.

Takenouchi now heard the whispers getting closer,

then hands were touching his body, trying to remove his armour and sword. Dropping his hand to his side he felt for his tanto (short dagger) and in a flash plunged it into the nearest looter. His scream put a fear beyond words into his comrades and they fled dropping their booty as they went. They knew that warrior spirits often haunted the battlefields, and their superstition was enough to allow Takenouchi to make good his escape.

Half staggering, half crawling, the wounded samurai left the field where so many of his friends had died. He knew he had to be quick because the jackals would be back. He managed to get to the forest and conceal himself in the thick undergrowth before he passed out.

When he came to he found himself in a cot with animal skins covering him. His eyes opened and looking down on him was a man of about sixty.

'Ah, you are awake my brave friend,' said the old man. 'Don't worry, you will live to fight another day. Your wound was in the flesh and I have managed to take out the arrowhead.' With that the old man turned away and moved to pass him something.

Takenouchi without thinking, for he was too weak to care, took from the old man a hot bowl of broth, sipping it at first until it cooled, then taking great gulps. It was just what he had needed. He then slumped back into the cot and fell asleep.

The following day Takenouchi, who now felt much better, learned that his benefactor was named Sato and that he was yamabushi (ascetic hermit warrior). The yamabushi, Takenouchi knew, were warriors that had for some reason tired of life and gone off to live in remote regions to study philosophy and practise Zen. Sato, he later found out, had been living in these particular foothills for over twenty years.

Within two weeks Takenouchi was fit and well, and each morning outside Sato's house he would practise his sword cuts to regain his skill. Sato would watch the warrior going through his paces, and commented that his shoulder was now almost like new again. In the evenings they would talk of bygone battles and techniques of warfare.

Sato explained that constant warfare had led him to search for something more than death and killing. He had retired from his lord's service and gone off to contemplate the meaning of existence and his relationship with the rest of the world. After ten years he knew he wanted to live alone for ever and never again have to kill anyone. The times, of course, being what they were there would always be a threat from robbers, bandits and anyone else who roamed the country looking to steal. So he had devised a fighting method to protect himself, but one which would not kill the adversary. He called this a 'gentler way' of handling dangerous situations. Takenouchi was curious and asked Sato to show him his method of fighting.

The old man said 'Grab me in a hold that you feel I cannot escape from.'

Obeying, Takenouchi executed a stranglehold but within a split second he was sent flying backwards and landed in a heap on the ground.

'Try harder!' Sato cried.

Takenouchi came running up in an attempt to knock the old man over. Instead, the samurai finished up in a clump of bushes.

'This time', the old man said, 'try to kill me.'

Takenouchi walked calmly over to Sato then hurled his whole body forwards to envelop the man in a vice-like grip. Seconds later he was again picking himself up from the ground and wiping the dust off his kimono.

'How is this possible?' asked Takenounchi. He was very perplexed that an old man had rendered him useless so easily.

'My gentle way', announced Sato, 'is based upon arresting techniques and using the energy and the strength of the opponent against them. I have wrestled with mountain bears and defeated them. But no one ever gets hurt, unless I want them to.'

For two years Takenouchi stayed with the old man and learned his mountain art of hand–to–hand fighting and throwing. Eventually, he felt it was time to leave and return to civilisation. He thanked Sato for everything he had done for him and for teaching him his art of the gentle way. Once he had returned home, to the amazement of his friends and family who had thought him dead, he gave up the sword and concentrated upon the gentle way of fighting that the old yamabushi had taught him. Years later, Takenouchi had devised an unarmed combat system inspired by Sato with further embellishments of his own. He named this system jiu–jitsu or 'gentle art'.

§

The Peasants Against an Empire

II

Throughout Southeast Asia, in times of trouble and war, it was always the peasants that answered their countries call to arms. The simple farmers would gather in village groups and head off in the direction of the fighting. Many kings of these countries kept armies, but these were usually for the defence of their own capital. So for centuries it was left to the people to defend their homeland themselves. Many never returned whilst others came back crippled and unable to work their fields. It therefore became customary to leave the eldest son at home as a kind of insurance policy.

One country that time and time again used these peasant armies was Burma, which is now called Myanmar (the original Burmese name for the country). The Burmese people had a martial art that was reputedly given to them by the gods called myanma letwhei. This martial art seemed to be a mixture of boxing, karate and kung fu. Southeast Asia was a melting pot of many cultures for half a millennium, and so it is reasonable to assume that the people of many lands settled up and down Burma.

The fighting arts first taught to the higher ranks of the army by the Ayegyi monks during the reign of King Anawratha were the letwhei, the bando (a softer blocking and countering art) and the naban (a form of grappling akin to wrestling). When they retired, many of the soldiers would go back to their home village and earn a living by teaching fighting skills. Gradually, this art became a sport much like the neighbouring kingdom of Siam's muay thai. In fact both countries clashed on many occasions, and the deciding factor in a battle would be a fight between the champions from each country.

Burma was mostly covered by thick impenetrable jungle and often lacked a proper army. Her warlike neighbours in what are present-day China, India, Bangladesh and Laos often invaded for no other reason than to take food and slaves, and also her seaports were being constantly raided by pirates. In response to all this a type of people's militia was formed.

Because it cost money to manufacture weapons, the simple peasant farmers had to rely on their letwhei skills and roughly made spears. In 1287 the great Kublai Khan's grandson Timur invaded Burma and destroyed the Pagan dynasty. Within a hundred years the constant battles between the people of Burma and Timur's soldiers led to Timur's descendants eventually withdrawing. The new dynasty of Toungoo was established and for 250 years fought battle after battle with border raiders and pirates. Whenever there was a battle the letwhei fighters could be found in the thick of it, leaping in the air with knee kicks to unseat armed horsemen and elbow smashes to the face. Their bravery at attempting to repel the enemy with just their bare hands and feet was incredible.

When there were no wars the various villages would set up letwhei matches between champion fighters. Every fighter wore a colourful tattoo on their thighs. This tattoo was a symbol of manhood and was a mandatory requirement for all letwhei fighters. Because most of the fighters were peasant farmers these contests could only be held during festivals and at harvest time. Some of the great champions would fight for money which would be shared by his whole village.

Then in 1824 the British came to Burma via India. In the battle for the coastal strip between Chittagong and Cape Negrais massed armies of peasants along with the king's troops fought long and hard against the might and firepower of the British army. The letwhei fighters were as always in the midst of the hand-to-hand grappling. This petty war, in the eyes of the British anyway, did not result in the easy outcome they had expected. The Burmese people, mostly the peasant army, paid for every mile the British took in blood. Consequently, the British sent to India for reinforcements and it was by sheer firepower alone that these bare-handed fighters were finally defeated. Two wars later and the British over-ran Burma, annexing it as an Indian province and ruling it until 1937 when it was made a crown colony.

Today, under the present government of Myanmar, letwhei is all but forgotten. However, the deadly empty-hand art, which the Burmese used to defend their land for so many centuries, is still taught in many remote villages and amongst jungle tribes.

§

Grand
Ultimate
Fist

Π

Tai chi chuan ('grand ultimate fist') is said to be the most highly developed of all the kung fu styles, hence its impressive name. Although it is a branch of the pugilistic arts, it paradoxically spurns the boxing tradition of strength and force. When an exponent of tai chi chuan meets an opponent who strikes at him, he yields and takes advantage of the opponent's momentum. The adversary, meeting no resistance, is pushed or pulled off balance and thrown to the ground. The tai chi combat fighter relies heavily on the ability to interpret strength and then anticipate the opponent's every move, moving before he does, but not moving if he doesn't.

Tai chi chuan is regarded by most as a physical exercise to promote health and, in some cases, longevity. The practice of tai chi (the more familiar name) in ancient times combined with special diets aided the Taoist priests in their search for immortality. There are many tai chi legends and stories about such people. The following is perhaps one of the more famous ones.

Long ago in Fukien province there was a priest who was taught his Tiger style kung fu by a monk who had reputedly fought a man-eating tiger and defeated it. The priest knew the system inside out and was now teaching a few select students in his village. One day he was travelling in the foothills, looking for herbs to stock up his medicine shelf, when he saw a particular flower whose petals could be used in a medication for acute chest pains. It was growing from the side of a ledge near the cliff edge. As he reached out to pluck it, he lost his footing and fell headlong down the side of the cliff, landing on a small ledge where he remained unconscious for several days.

When he eventually came to he found himself on this precarious perch, which had broken his fall and saved him from crashing to his death on the rocks hundreds of feet below. His degree of pain and hunger told him that he had been unconscious for quite a time. No one knew where he was and having neither food nor water the priest knew his demise was almost certain. Further up the ledge he spied an opening in the cliff, which looked like the mouth of a small cave. He slowly crawled along the ledge and saw that it was indeed a cave, so he crawled in.

He slept for a long time, his body wracked with pain and his strength diminishing hour by hour due to hunger. He awoke at about noon the next day. Accepting the fact that all was lost he decided to spend the time he had left in deep Taoist meditation. At least with this he could rise above the pain that by now was his constant companion. As he looked around the small cave he noticed what looked like a skeleton in the corner. Moving over he saw the remains of what had been a man, and around the waist hung a small leather pouch. He removed the pouch and opened it to find faded documents that were barely legible.

For the rest of the day he read what he could of the faded pages. He found that the name of the deceased person was Chan Sang Feng and he had discovered a method for both fighting and physical well-being. Various diagrams of body movements were included in the notes, plus advice upon healing through a series of deep breathing exercises. With nothing else to do, the priest followed the instructions. Each day he went through the same exercises but still nothing seemed to be happening. At least a heavy rainstorm some days before had allowed him to quench his thirst.

One morning he awoke and was about to continue with the exercises and the breathing techniques when he heard sounds coming from outside the cave. He shouted for help several times before a voice answered back. A few minutes later what appeared to be a hunter stood at the mouth of the cave. The priest explained what had happened and how he fell. The hunter told him he was lucky to be discovered; they had shot a bird in flight and it had fallen on the ledge that led to the cave. The bird was too big to let go so they had climbed down to the ledge to retrieve it and heard him shout.

The hunter with help from his friends eventually succeeded in getting the priest back up the cliff. They asked him where he had come from and he told them it was a village some distance to the south called Chen. They helped him aboard their cart and headed in the direction the priest had indicated and reached the village two days later. People came out to welcome the strangers but upon seeing the priest fled screaming back into their homes. Eventually, the village mayor came out and spoke to the very puzzled hunters. Upon hearing a familiar voice, the priest looked up and said hello. The mayor just stared unbelievably at the priest and said, 'Where have you been for the last two months? Everyone here thought you dead.'

Sul
Sa

П

One of the most feared fighters in the Orient was the Korean Sul Sa. They were contemporaries of Japan's ninja clans, but their aims and moral values were quite different. The ninja only fought for money, but the Sul Sa were trained to defend their country and people. They were formed just over 900 years ago to be the eyes and ears of the kingdom of Koguryo and its weapon of retribution.

During the reign of King Tae Cho Wang, Koguryo's main enemies were the Chinese and Mongols. Survival of the kingdom depended solely on the people's ability to repel the constant attacks. A group of highly trained fighters was formed at this time called the Sun Bae. These warriors were hand-picked from those who fought in battle with great valour and an indomitable spirit. The three most notable characteristics of the Sun Bae were their ability to face death with an almost reckless indifference, their high degree of skill with weapons and empty-hand fighting and also a deep sense of honour.

When a massed army of Chinese and Mongols arrived on the borders of the kingdom, every able-bodied citizen was mobilised to face this great peril. The generals knew that they were heavily outnumbered and the only way to gain an advantage against their enemy was off the battlefield. So one general came up with the idea of a contest, much like the Olympic Games, but fighting arts were to be included. All the warriors of the Sun Bae were invited to take part. The general's idea was to use the games as an elimination process, so that they would finish up with the very best of the best warriors.

Thousands of the Sun Bae attended this week-long contest, and it is said that their campfires illuminated the countryside for more than a hundred miles. The general needed about a thousand men for what he had in mind, so as the games progressed each contest was taken to a final and great athletes and fighters alike were either chosen or passed over. Eventually, there were just over 2500 warriors to choose from.

The last contest involved playing tjyang-keui, which is a variant of the game of chess, and pa-tok, which is a game played with pebbles on a board, similar to the Japanese game of Go.

The general in his wisdom knew that the very cream of the martial arts fighters were gathered before him, but, as well as warrior skills, the members of the special force he had in mind to create would need intelligence. He announced that the winners of the two board games would be the overall winners of the contest. By early evening he had assembled the final victors of the games, which numbered just over 1100 men. He then informed the group that he was setting up a special force to be called the Sul Sa and this force would be the vanguard of Koguryo's army.

The next task was to separate all the married men from the single men, then to separate all the married men with families from the married men without families. The training for the whole group would be the same, but in the face of certain death in the field it would be the Sul Sa with nothing to lose who would be the bravest. A married man with or without a family would think just that little bit differently when all hope was gone.

Everyone in the unit was taught to follow the principles of harmony and to be in tune with nature, because when they were out in the field on a mission their surroundings would be their friend and nature would be their only ally.

Within a year the first groups were ready to go into battle. The war had not been going well for Koguryo and many good men had been lost in battle. The Chinese and Mongols had made many conquests and the situation was looking dire. The first groups of Sul Sa went out on spying expeditions to gather information about their enemy's weak and strong points. Other groups were involved in sabotage and the issuing of false information.

One special group was only concerned with assassination. These Sul Sa would wait for days around enemy encampments, just looking, waiting and listening, seeing who gave the orders and identifying the chain of command. Once they had discovered all they needed to know, they would creep into the encampment at night and murder the captains, generals and chiefs in their beds, then disappear as silently as they had come.

This particular section of the Sul Sa had far more effect upon the enemy than even they thought possible. The enemy blamed demons, the gods, in fact anything that came to mind but not the Sul Sa. Whole armies were left without commanders of any expertise. The battalions looked to the lower-ranking officers for orders, but in those days these were of peasant stock and not great thinkers. They needed the officers and leaders from the nobility to issue commands that they could trust and so follow. They were left to work things out for themselves which led to dissension within the ranks.

In fewer than three months the invasion had become a rout, thanks to the daring exploits of this incredible body of men. History does not record the name of the general who first organised the Sul Sa into a fighting force, but thanks to his far-sighted thinking the kingdom of Koguryo was saved from the Chinese. Such was the impact of the general's strategy that many of today's special forces units were inspired by his example.

Jam
Pon
Ken
Π

The two karate fighters swiftly moved backwards and forwards across the dojo ('training hall'). First one would kick and the opponent would block and retaliate with a counter blow. The students watching this exhibition were cheering for their favourite. After about two minutes the fight ended with the senior student of the two, a boy named Tatso, declared the winner. The crowd dispersed and Tatso went to wipe himself down.

The sensei ('teacher') of the school, who had also been watching the fight, walked over to Tatso and said, 'Tell me Tatso, why do you always choose Yasu-jiro to fight with?'

'Because sensei,' replied the boy, 'Yasujiro and myself are the two best fighters in the school. I know I am his senior and that is why I always win. But the other students love to see us sparring and I feel it gives them something to aim for in their training.'

'Nice sentiments Tatso, and I admire your concern for your fellow students' way. [Way is what *do* means in karate. The way is the journey one takes when training in martial arts. For instance, karate-do means 'way of karate', judo means 'the gentle way' and kendo 'the way of the sword'.] But it is also your journey too. How will you feel when Yasujiro finally beats you in a match?'

'How can that happen sensei? Especially when I will always be ahead of Yasujiro in training.'

'The day will come when Yasujiro discovers your method for winning,' replied the sensei.

'But by that time I will have progressed further and my experience will be the greater,' stated Tatso.

'Who is to say which of you will be the better fighter?' asked the sensei. 'At the moment you both fight with love in your hearts for each other. If the fight was for real, with hate in one or the other's heart, the result would be different. Then the sensei enquired, 'Do you know the children's game of jam-pon-ken [scissors, stone, paper]?'

'Yes,' replied Tatso, 'I do. I played it many times when I was a child.'

'And did you win?'

'Sometimes.'

'Do you think you could beat Yasujiro at this game?'

'Why of course I could,' replied Tatso.

'Why of course?' asked the sensei.

'Because it is a game of strategy and being the best fighter and the older student my intelligence and wits are much sharper,' replied Tatso.

The teacher called for Yasujiro to come to him. Seconds later Yasujiro appeared at the door of the dojo.

'Yasujiro,' the teacher said, 'I have been talking with Tatso and we feel there is only room for one of you at my school. I think it would be unfair to ask you to leave just because you are the lesser trained of the two of you. So I have decided that you will play the game of jam-pon-ken with Tatso, and whichever of you loses will leave the karate school for ever', lied the sensei.

Upon hearing this Yasujiro went pale. The thought of never again training in karate with the master upset him deeply. A sullen-looking Yasujiro nodded his assent and the game began.

After about nine games Tatso who was winning then began to lose. After thirteen games Tatso was back on top and in front. After thirty games each one was winning every other game,

'Stop!' the sensei suddenly shouted. 'That is enough.'

He then went on to tell Yasujiro, who was at this point behind in the score, that it was just a cruel joke. But he had done it to give Yasujiro the intent and force of mind to win at any cost. A very relieved Yasujiro nodded to his teacher and went off smiling.

'So,' the sensei said. 'Did you learn anything from the game you have just played Tatso?'

'Yes sensei,' replied Tatso. 'I have learned that because Yasujiro was put under pressure to win and I was not, he played a much more thinking game than I did. I was winning for a time but then Yasujiro watched my random moves and obviously began to calculate which of the three, stone, paper, scissors, I used the most and countered it.'

The sensei smiled and said, 'Tatso I am pleased you understood what has just happened. Also you now understand my earlier point about always fighting with the same opponent.'

'Thank you sensei,' the boy replied. 'I do know now what you meant and things will be different from now on.'

'Let me leave you with an old proverb Tatso, which will remind you of this incident: "Do not fight too often with one enemy, or you will teach him all your art of war." '

Upon hearing this the boy smiled and walked off. Just as he bowed before he left the dojo the sensei shouted to him.

'By the way Tatso, do not be too disappointed with your little game of jam-pon-ken. Although you would have won if you had played longer, Yasujiro would have won had you played even longer, and you would have won again if you had played longer again. You see, with the game of jam-pon-ken no one ever wins outright because mathematically it is impossible!'

§

The Unseen Fan

Π

In a small town in northern India a young man named Han Ming had grown up learning the sword arts of his father. Originally from China, Ming's father had travelled to India and settled there. He was peerless as a kung fu fighter and a master of weapons. So, quite naturally, his only son Han Ming was brought up from a very early age learning everything about the martial arts. By the time he was twenty, as well as the empty-hand arts he was also a master of swordplay. Being still young and adventurous, he wandered about determined to seek out formidable opponents to test his skill, with the hope of perfecting his already superb ability. Unbeaten in his homeland, Han decided to travel to China to test his skills against the Chinese systems. He felt that the land of his forebears would have much to offer in this area if his father's stories were to believed.

Bidding farewell to his family, he set off on the great trek across the mountains and down into China. As he travelled he met and crossed blades with several famous swordsmen, beating them all. Once he even went into a brigand stronghold to meet the leader of a gang of robbers because he had heard that the man was highly skilled with the broadsword. Suffice to say the robber leader was no match for Han, and when he left the hideout the robbers were drawing lots for a new leader.

This period of 'testing' his skills drew much attention to Han as a fighter. He began to find that his name was already known as a great sword fighter when he entered towns and villages on his journey. After ten years of never being beaten and shedding much blood in the process, Han thought that he should reflect upon his next course of action. There is an old proverb which states, 'Why fight a man you know you can beat; what is to be achieved from the outcome?' Feeling that this 'testing of the blade' was now becoming tiresome, he disappeared into the mountains for a number of years to meditate. He came to the conclusion that he should settle down and marry.

He married a Chinese girl who bore him a son. He taught his son everything he knew about fighting and the use of the sword, just as his father had done years before. Unfortunately, Han's son's disposition was not like that of his own. As the boy grew to manhood his recklessness combined with his arrogance resulted in the deaths of many challengers. Around the countryside the son's quick temper caused many challenges to be issued and always with the same result. He had inherited all his father's skill but none of his wisdom.

Han Ming thought he would teach the boy a lesson and so publicly challenged his son to a duel. However, to his dismay, his son had learned well the art of the sword and knew all the tricks his father would use to defeat him. The fight went on for a long time and the best Han Ming could do was to bring the duel to a stalemate. The idea of embarrassing his son had not worked. The son, now knowing that he was the equal of his father even at his young age, went from bad to worse.

Han decided that a period of meditation was needed to discover what his next course of action should be in his attempt to teach his son the value of life. It was the height of summer and even though it was cooler in the mountains Han was bothered by the flies that seemed to always be around him. So he constructed a fan to help keep the flies at bay whilst he pondered upon his problem.

Day after day Han sat and reflected, swishing the flies away continuously. It was then he had an amazing thought; by continually swishing away the flies he realised what deft hand movements were needed to do this. The weeks passed and the seasons changed. It was now winter and the first flakes of snow began to settle upon the Jade Mountain, which had been Han's home during his contemplation. Han had constructed an iron fan which could be easily handled in combat. Once he had a working model he then set about inventing a theory and practice for the use of such a weapon.

He devised seven techniques that would lock a sword in combat. Then he went further and found a method of using the fan for close fighting and for striking nerve points on the body. His principle was that if he moved in very close, almost crowding a fighter, the longer reach of a sword blade would be rendered useless. He named his technique the White Jade Fan after the mountain where he had stayed and the snow that fell as he had finally discovered an answer to his problem.

Publicly announcing a return match, Han and his son again faced each other in the town square for a duel. Only this time Han countered his son's every move. He used the techniques he had formulated on the mountain, and fought his son to a standstill. By using intricate footwork patterns, he then managed to get inside his son's defence and strike a disarming nerve blow. The sword dropped to the floor and the son could do nothing but concede victory to his father. Han had actually only used six of his seven techniques. The seventh was a deadly nerve strike to a part of the body that would cause death in an instant. He was thankful he had not had to use it on his son.

However, the story, alas, does not have a happy ending. The son was so incensed at being publicly humiliated by his father that he became even more aggressive and killed many people. Han, not wanting his new style to perish, took on a student to learn the system he had created, so that after his own death the student would always be there to intervene when Han's son attempted to hurt anyone. As for the secret seventh technique, that unfortunately died with Han Ming. He could not teach it to his student, for fear that at some later date he would use it to kill his son.

§

The Shaolin Legacy

II

The story of how the Shaolin Temple in Honan province, northern China was attacked and burnt down, with most of the monks massacred and only a few managing to escape, has long been a kung fu legend. But why was the temple destroyed and what of the aftermath?

The impact of martial artists on the course of Chinese history has been profound. Kung fu practitioners have made their mark not only as monks and soldiers, but as rebels and members of secret societies as well. The existence of secret societies devoted to political struggle and martial arts training goes back hundreds of years. In the 1300s the White Lotus society played a major part in the Red Turban rebellion which overthrew Mongolian rule and installed the Ming dynasty, which flourished until the Manchu invasion in the 17th century.

The Manchus were also known as the Ching and were essentially non-Chinese nomads from Manchuria. This Manchu invasion and the subsequent establishment of the Ching dynasty, which was to last for the next three hundred years, was deeply hated throughout China. Immensely disliked by the common people, the Manchu government retaliated with unjust laws and taxation. This brought about a rapid growth in underground societies.

The Manchus were also aware that in times of great strife and trouble the ordinary peasant farmer turned to the monks and priests for help. Fearing the influence of the Shaolin Temple as a centre of revolutionaries, the Manchu rulers destroyed the temple, killing all but a few. The survivors, now known as the 'five ancestors', spread their art of kung fu and their politics throughout China. They devoted themselves totally to the destruction of the hated Manchus. Their battle cry was, 'Overthrow the Ching and restore the Ming'. The secret societies that now flourished in 17th-century China were to grow and become the modern Triad and Tong organisations of today. One leader in the anti-Ching movement, decades later, became a leader of 20th-century Chinese politics, Dr Sun Yat-sen. He was the first president of the republic of China.

Martial arts training in both kung fu and weapons was never more widely available than during the 18th and 19th centuries. Monks from many of the other fighting temples, which had been established all over China, were now teaching farmers and merchants alike the principles of killing and how to overcome an adversary simply by using empty hands. This was an age of rebellion and down the years that followed the people wanted to be ready to rise up and challenge the Manchus. Unfortunately, other factors were at work beyond their control.

By the first half of the 19th century foreign 'white devils' were making inroads into China in the name of trade. The British forced the unwilling Chinese to engage in trade and then retaliated with gunboats and war when the Manchu rulers tried to stop the illegal, but rapidly growing, opium trade. The anti-Ching rebels suddenly looked upon their Manchu overlords as not being quite so bad as they had first thought. The result of the escalating conflict with the British were the so-called Opium Wars. The disastrous effects of the war and the unequal treaty the Manchu government had been forced to sign by the British led to China's economic collapse. The burden of all this fell, as usual, upon the backs of the peasants.

The only line of action now open for the lower classes was war, and so rebellion and revolts spread throughout China. Foreign troops of the Western powers were continually being attacked by Chinese fighting with bare hands. Never in the whole history of martial arts the world over has kung fu and its related weapons systems been used to such an advantage by so many.

Of all the rebellions that took place, save for the Boxer Uprising, none was more bloodthirsty or so costly of human life than the Taiping Rebellion. Some estimate that more than 15 million people were killed in this insurrection. The revolt was led by a man from a respected martial arts background named Hung Hsiu-chuan. His hidden agenda included radical land reform and redistribution of wealth. Of course the merchants and ruling classes got very nervous when they heard his political programme and sought help from the Manchu government, who in their turn solicited military aid from the Western powers, which they were only too happy to provide.

Thousand upon thousand of martial artists took part in the rebellion. Masters and students fought side by side against the Manchus and Western powers. But the superiority of Western firepower won the day. The Taiping Rebellion was suppressed. The Manchus had survived but now China was completely at the mercy of the Western powers. Millions of peasants had been killed and those that survived faced a life of poverty.

The Triad societies and anti-foreign secret societies, however, grew tremendously. The masters of the martial arts and their students regrouped and reorganised, and continued training so that if they were needed in the future to again rally in defence of their homeland, they would be ready. A few decades later they were needed, during the storm that was the Boxer Uprising.

Master
of
Shuriken

Π

The master of the sword at Kimura Castle was a certain Ishimoto. He was quite concerned by a letter he had received in which he was being challenged to a duel. Normally, Ishimoto would not have been worried but the challenger was Fujisaki Kase.

Kase had sought out two of Ishimoto's friends earlier in the month and challenged them both to duels. In each case Kase had won the fights and killed both men. He had gained the advantage in the fight by striking at his opponent's sword very hard and breaking it clean in two.

Ishimoto remembered that there were stories about a fighter roaming the countryside and only fighting swordmasters. In each case this fighter had broken his opponent's weapon with his own mighty sword before he cleaved his adversary in two. The people had labelled this sword the Rock-shattering Widowmaker. Ishimoto was now feeling his own sword and wondering if it could stand up to Kase's. Although his weapon had been made by one of the finest sword smiths in Japan and had been used in many famous battles, Ishimoto still worried whether the blade could withstand Kase's mighty blows with the Widowmaker.

The next day Ishimoto and Kase met at a clearing in the woods where the duel would be fought. The two men squared off and prepared to do battle. They slowly moved around each other, never for a moment taking their eyes off one another. Ishimoto was eager to be finished so that he could go back to the castle, so he made the first move which was deftly blocked. Going in with a further attack Ishimoto swung the sword upwards which was parried at the last moment by Kase. The block was so strong that Ishimoto's sword broke in half. Before he could recover Kase cut his opponent down and killed him.

With the famous Ishimoto dead, Kase now felt ready to challenge Yagu Mitsuyoshi, who was the swordmaster and instructor to the shogun himself. He thought that when he killed Yagu the shogun would promote him to the position of swordmaster, which would make him both rich and famous. During his journey to the school of Master Yagu at Edo

Castle, Kase was already thinking what he was going to do with all the money he would earn. Some days later he arrived at the fencing school of Master Yagu.

Master Yagu looked a strange sight for a great master, as he walked with a limp and had a patch over his eye. He had lost the eye in a great battle some years earlier. He doesn't look much, thought Kase when he came upon Yagu. Master Yagu had been expecting his challenger for some time now. The stories about Kase and his great sword had reached Yagu, and aspiring fighters, sooner or later, always wanted to take on the shogun's swordmaster. Over the years a steady stream of challengers had knocked at his door, eager to challenge him, but all had been sent away beaten. However, Kase had also defeated everyone he had fought.

'My name is Fujisaki Kase,' the swordsman said, 'and I have come to challenge you to a duel.'

Yagu smiled, then turned and called out, 'Gentatsu come here.'

A young man of about twenty-five years old entered the room. He was a cripple and depended upon a crutch to keep him upright.

'My man Gentatsu will fight you,' Yagu declared.

'How can this cripple fight against me?' Fujisaki demanded.

'He has mastered the essential principles of the martial arts, and I have great faith in him. If you can defeat him, then I'll fight you,' Yagu answered.

Kase knew that he had no choice but to slay the cripple. So they arranged to meet at noon the next day. Kase then left the castle very annoyed that he should have to go through an intermediary before he could kill Yagu.

At the appointed time, Yagu and the cripple Gentatsu met Kase in the courtyard where the duel was to take place.

'Now cripple,' Kase shouted, 'I am about to put you out of your misery.'

Gentatsu was just propping himself up against the wall, he put aside his crutch and then hobbled awkwardly towards Kase. The swordsman come rushing at him with his huge sword raised above his head. Gentatsu with amazing speed jumped to one side and his hands seemed to move in a blur. Seconds later Kase fell to the ground dead, with twenty-two shuriken (sharp-pointed throwing stars, much favoured by the ninja) embedded in his chest. The speed with which Gentatsu had thrown them gave one the notion that they had all been joined together.

'Come Gentatsu,' said Yagu 'We will take some drink and reflect upon the day's events.'

'Yes master,' said Gentatsu. 'When will these people ever learn that the shogun would not just hire a swordmaster merely to teach him to fence. A man of such importance needs to know how all weapons are used that is why he hires us ninja to teach him these things.'

§

The Deceptive Arrows

Π

During the period in China known as the Warring States, three kingdoms fought for supremacy. Many battles took place during this time and the balance of power shifted constantly from one kingdom to another with neither really gaining complete superiority.

In the kingdom of Wei, the war was going rather badly and shortages in both food and weapons were now beginning to tell. The general in command of the armed forces held a war council with his captains, asking each of them to come up with ideas to combat the shortages. After a few hours it was decided that the major shortfall was arrows.

'If we are to defend the city successfully', said the general, 'then I need at least one hundred thousand arrows.'

Deep gasps came from the assembled officers, because one hundred thousand arrows would take months to make, and already the armies of the kingdom of Wu were assembling just on the other side of the river.

'What are we to do?' cried one of the captains.

Another voiced his opinion which was that they were doomed and that they should surrender to the king of Wu and perhaps prevent a massacre. Some of the other captains agreed with this suggestion.

Just then Lin Ku, the king's philosopher, walked into the war council meeting to tell the general that the king had urgent need of him.

'You have a great problem I fear,' said Lin Ku.

The general looked at the philosopher, whom he did not particularly like, for even though he was the finest martial artist in the kingdom he had retired to seek enlightenment.

'We have no arrows with which to fight the enemy,' said the general. 'What do you suggest we do about it philosopher?' the general said somewhat sarcastically.

'I would perhaps suggest reflecting upon the problem, for within every problem lie the seeds of its solution,' replied Lin Ku.

'I need one hundred thousand arrows in ten days or the kingdom is lost,' retorted the general. 'So unless you are a magician as well as a philosopher, I suggest you keep your adages to yourself.'

Lin Ku responded tersely, 'Fighting is more than just a clashing of armed troops. Fighting is about understanding, knowing your enemy and knowing yourself. If these two concepts are followed, then you will be the victor of a thousand battles. So, general, I advise that you look to strategy as your saviour. One good plan is worth more than a thousand ideas.'

'If you are so knowledgeable philosopher, then you find me the arrows!' answered the general angrily. 'In fact, after all you have said, if you don't find me the arrows in ten days then I will inform the king you have been meddlesome and you can look to him for punishment.'

'General,' said Lin Ku, 'I will bring you the arrows in five days!' He left the room to roars of laughter as this would be an impossibility.

Lin Ku was given twelve soldiers to help him with his task. For two days and two nights he just sat around not seeming to care about the task assigned to him. The soldiers reported back to the general each day as to Lin Ku's progress

'He does nothing but sit around all day,' said one soldier to the general. Another commented, 'He eats, he drinks and he tends his garden'. The general listened and knew that Lin Ku could not possibly fulfil the order in time. He would now be able to have his revenge on the pompous philosopher.

In the late afternoon of the third day, Lin Ku requested a fleet of river barges be made ready. He then ordered that huge bales of hay be placed inside the barges so that they completely covered the whole of the deck area. As evening came Lin Ku, the twelve soldiers assigned to him and the bargemen set forth across the river. Quizzical looks were passed from one soldier to another. No one could understand what was happening. Halfway across the river a dense fog came in and settled. By now the barges were nearing the far bank, where the army of Wu was encamped. The soldiers on the barges began to feel a little uncomfortable at being so close to an army of fifty thousand men.

Lin Ku came out on deck and ordered every man on all the barges to shout and scream for all they were worth and then to take cover below. Not understanding what was transpiring the soldiers obeyed then rushed for cover. The noise of the shouting carried across to the enemy encampment. A captain came rushing into the tent of the commander and said that the crafty army of Wei had decided to attack under the cover of fog. The commander ordered all the archers to the bank and to the cliff edge. He told them to fire into the bank of fog which is where the enemy was hiding.

'A shower of arrows cascading down upon them will put an end to their attempt to surprise us,' said the commander.

Within two minutes twenty thousand bowmen were firing their deadly missiles at the fog bank. Meanwhile on the barges the arrows whistled through he air and found homes in their unseen target, the bales of hay. For half an hour or so wave upon wave of enemy arrows showered down on to the barges and embedded themselves in the bales of hay.

Lin Ku went back on deck and ordered the barges to be returned to their own side of the river. Daylight was just breaking through the clouds as they arrived back. The barges looked like porcupines with so many arrows sticking out of the bales.

'We must have in excess of two hundred thousand arrows here,' remarked Lin Ku. 'Remove them all and take them in wagons to the general with my compliments, and say to him: a reflection upon a pool of water does not reveal its depth; so too it is with men!'

§

The Strategy of War

Π

About 300 years ago, towards the end of the Ming dynasty, an unknown scholar wrote a book comprising of thirty-six stratagems for the waging of war. The book focuses upon using deception and subterfuge to achieve military objectives. The title of the book is simply *The 36 Stratagems*, and has been likened to Sun Tsu's great work on the same subject, *The Art of War*. The author of the stratagems conceded that as long as human nature does not change, war will continue to follow certain patterns which can be observed by a discerning mind. The applications of the thirty-six stratagems is not limited to the battlefield but can be applied to everyday situations as well.

In the practice of martial arts when two opponents are of equal skill and training, then it is the one that uses the best strategy who will be the victor. As it is in the martial ways, so it is in war. Be quick to exploit any weakness of your enemy or opponent. Any oversight of theirs must be looked upon as an opportunity for you. Most military strategists of any worth in ancient China were also philosophers and highly skilled in the martial arts. Constant training in a martial arts discipline hones the mind as well as the body. The practitioner develops a kind of sixth sense in which he can see beyond an immediate situation. He can, as we say today, 'look at the big picture'. It can be best summed up in the proverb: 'You may be my brother but I can see through thirteen walls.'

In the year 770 BC, the Duke of Sheng joined forces with another province in an attempt to overcome the powerful kingdom of Song. Alarmed at finding a mighty army on his borders the King of Song asked his ministers for advice. It was advised that if he took most of his army in secret to the Duke's stronghold and attacked it, then with so few of the Duke's soldiers left guarding his home he would be forced to return to save it.

So the King, after securing help from another province, led his army in the attack on the duke's castle. He was successful in his plan. The invasion of Sheng forced the Duke to break off the intended attack on Song and return home to rescue his state. The King now satisfied that the strategy had worked was about to march home when it was brought to his attention that by making a slight detour they would pass through the land of Dai. They could eliminate this city and so stop it from ever becoming a threat in the future. So the King laid siege to the city of Dai.

Meanwhile, the ministers of Dai had sent out messengers to the duke of Sheng informing him of their plight and requesting help. The Duke ordered his great army to the rescue of the city. When the generals of Dai saw the Duke's army approaching they flung open the gates to admit them and knew they had been saved. But the Duke had other ideas, once in the city his army overran the Dai army and forced them to surrender, which they had no choice but to do.

The King of Song, when he heard how the duke's army had just entered the city and captured it, just as he was about to lay siege, became enraged.

'We took the trouble to attack Dai and he reaps the benefit.'

Now, of course, the balance of power had changed, and the Sheng army combined with the Dai army was far superior to the Song army, and so the king had to call off the siege and return home with no honours.

The stratagem here is: benefit from the toil of others. This can be used when the enemy exposes an unexpected flaw, then one must act quickly to take advantage of the opportunity for victory.

§

The Kung Fu Fisherman

Π

In the small town of Jenshou in Fukien province there lived a retired kung fu master of the White Crane system. He had been a great sifu ('teacher') in his younger days but had suddenly stopped teaching to follow a different course in life. His senior students went their different ways, teaching what they knew of the White Crane. The most senior student had expected to gain the secret knowledge of the fighting system, which as tradition dictated would have been just before the master died. But his sifu had not died but retired, so, disillusioned, he sought to learn another style from a master beyond the mountains.

The retired sifu, who was called Lung Ti, spent all his days fishing and philosophising. Everyday, whilst he was on the riverbank, a young boy of about sixteen years old would pass him by and wish him good day. Lung Ti thought him a pleasant fellow as most of the town's youth were rowdy and followed the ways of drunkenness. One particular day, the boy did not appear, nor the next day. After about a week Lung Ti became a little concerned, so he made it his business to find out what had become of the youth.

Initial inquiries led him to a small cottage on the edge of the forest, which was said to be the youth's home. His sick mother answered the knock on the door and invited Lung Ti in. He then heard of how on a regular basis the youths of the town would attack the boy, whose name was Pang Ji, and beat him up. This had been going on for years, but it had not deterred the brave boy from travelling into the town to earn a meagre pittance to help feed himself and his mother. Lung informed the boy that when he had recovered from his latest beating he should come and see him as he had work for him.

Three weeks later Pang Ji went to Lung's home, fully recovered and ready to work. The old master took the boy to the riverbank and gave him a rod and told him to fish.

The boy obeyed without question, but after about an hour he asked Lung, 'Is this my work, that you are going to pay me for, just sitting here fishing all day?'

'Yes,' replied Lung, 'this is what you must do.'

Around dusk, the old master picked up his rod and

the fish they had both caught and went home to cook them. He paid Pang Ji his wages for the day and invited him to stay for supper. The boy nodded and the pair ate an enjoyable meal.

Before the boy went home Lung said to him, 'There is a proverb which sates: give a man a fish and he is fed for a day, teach him to fish and he is fed for a lifetime.' The boy nodded and Lung continued, 'These boys in the town have given you a hard time for years yet you do not complain. Why is this?'

The boy replied, 'Because, sir, there is nothing I can do about it. They are many and stronger than me.'

Lung listened and then told the boy what he used to be before he took up fishing. He added that starting from tomorrow he would train Pang in the system of the White Crane.

Pang proved to be an exceptional student. Less than a year later Lung sent the boy into town on an errand. Pang left to fulfil his master's wish. The town rowdies who had not seen Pang Ji for quite some time approached him as he came into the town. Two of them lashed out at him for no other reason than to hurt the boy and to make the others all laugh. Pang just kept walking towards his destination, parrying the kicks with a circular block that put the two youths on their backs. The rest of the group ran after Pang and attempted to jump on him. Bodies suddenly started to fly around all over the place. One youth was thrown through the baker's window, another was thrown through a bamboo fence and finished up in the pigpen. Two more were dropped where they stood.

Pang finished the errand and turned to walk out of town. The youths were just beginning to come round, and when they saw Pang they gave him a very wide berth. One beating was enough for them. Arriving back at Lung's house, Pang told his master what had occurred.

Lung stared at the boy and said, 'You see Pang, I have now taught you to fish. You can now set up a kwoon ('school') in the town and teach kung fu for the rest of your life. Your mother and yourself will never go hungry again.'

Pang's kung fu school was a great success, especially since the old master had taught the boy every secret of the White Crane system.

§

Epilogue

A lthough many of the stories in this book are a
mix of fact and fable, the underlying theme I
hope the reader will grasp is that the martial arts and
the martial ways are merely a vehicle to guide the
inner being towards a realm of a deeper understanding of oneself. Many practitioners of martial arts ini-
tially take them up to learn how to fight. But then
the strange paradox occurs, namely the more one
knows how to fight the less one is inclined to do so.
The path of life parallels the 'Way' in the martial arts.
Both are journeys that can be fraught with fear. But
inner fears are merely shadows that fall away in the
light of greater awareness. So let the seeds of our des-
tiny be nourished by the experiences of our past. And
remember the Chinese proverb: 'The man who
removes a mountain begins by carrying away small
stones.'

Peter Lewis